MW00650300

Trellis Craft

HOW TO MAKE YOUR OWN COPPER PIPE GARDEN ORNAMENTS

written and illustrated by
Roger A. Beebe

Trellis Craft
PO Box 17000
Memphis TN 38187-1000

Trellis Craft – How to Make Your Own Copper Pipe Garden Ornaments. Copyright © 2003 by Roger A. Beebe. Printed and bound in the United States of America. All rights reserved. No part of this book may be reproduced in any form or by any electronic or mechanical means including information storage and retrieval systems without permission in writing from the publisher, except by a reviewer, who may quote brief passages in a review. Published by Trellis Craft, PO Box 17000, Memphis, TN 38187-1000.

First Edition January 2003. Second Printing September 2004.

Notice of Disclaimer

In preparing **Trellis Craft – How to Make Your Own Copper Pipe Garden Ornaments,** the author has attempted to make these projects as safe and successful as possible. The author is not an engineer, nor a professional of any type and makes no claim to be an expert in any area. Neither Trellis Craft nor the author nor sellers intend by this publication to explain all possible dangers known or unknown that may exist if any tool or project in this book is made or used. They do not assume any responsibility for any damages or injuries incurred in connection with the use of this manual.

The use of this material or information shall be solely at the user's own risk. The author, publisher, and sellers assume no responsibility or liability for the accuracy, fitness, proper design, safety, or safe use of any information, technique, tool, design, materials, use, etc. contained in **Trellis Craft – How to Make Your Own Copper Pipe Garden Ornaments**.

The reader waives any and all liability, damages, causes of action, claims, etc. against the author, publisher, or sellers resulting from any personal injury, wrongful death, or property damage resulting from the use or application of any design, technique, process, or other information contained herein.

ISBN 0-9727691-0-2

Please direct all correspondence to:

Trellis Craft

PO Box 17000

Memphis TN 38187-1000

(901) 682-0961

Or visit the Trellis Craft web site for online tips, techniques, and E-mail answers to your questions:

www.trelliscraft.com

Contents

CHAPTER 1 | *Getting Started*

Some tips to help you get the most out of this book and find what you need to get started.

How to Use this Book

This book may seem intimidating at first, full of unfamiliar terms, tools you have never used, and projects that seem difficult or complicated at first glance. If this is your feeling, here's how you can proceed:

1. Casually look through this book, without really trying to learn anything. Get a feel for what the book is about and what kinds of projects you can make

2. Let your imagination go to work. Maybe you will think "Hey, if I made a trellis like that, I'd have a place to grow one of those flowering vines I've been wanting to try!", or "wouldn't that project be a useful thing to have in my garden!"

3. If one of your imaginary projects seems especially interesting to you, then make actually doing it your goal. If it is a complicated project, it doesn't have to be your very first project. But every simple project you complete will help you accomplish the more complicated project later.

4. Now that you have a goal in mind, learn the things you need to know in order to accomplish your goal. Actually, there are only a few things you need to know:

   • Names of pipe and fittings and what you need to buy.

   • Tools and supplies you need.

   • How to measure and cut pipe.

   • How to use the tools to assemble the cut pipe and fittings.

That's it. There are chapters at the beginning of this book on these subjects. Read them over, get your materials together, and make a simple project. I guarantee that once your first project is complete and you are using it in your garden, you won't need any further encouragement to make more!

Along the way, this book has some guides to make finding information easy:

In This Chapter	**At the start of each chapter, this note summarizes what the chapter is about.**
Safety!	Read these safety notes to ensure you have a safe and pleasant experience building copper garden structures.
Tip	These special tips will help you work smarter, save time or money, or enjoy what you have made.
Note	To draw your attention to something important that you may otherwise overlook.

And remember, this book has an **index** to help you find the information you are looking for.

Keep It Simple at First

In the interest of completeness, this book has lots of more "advanced" information on working with copper pipe, such as making jigs and bending pipe.

When you first start, you can ignore all of the more advanced stuff, and just put together some simple projects using straight pipe. Check out **"First Projects"** on page 63.

For instance, most anybody could use a simple "pot trellis" to grow a small vine in a pot. A simple pot trellis consists of three pieces of pipe and two fittings — you can't get much simpler than that.

After you have some simple projects under your belt, come back and read the more advanced information and it probably won't seem quite so complicated.

Fast Start

Some people like to dive right in and start making projects without doing a lot of reading. If that is you, see these pages:

For the pipe and fittings you need for most projects: page 8.

For the tools and supplies you need for most projects: page 15.

For easy projects to start with: **"First Projects"** on page 63.

CHAPTER 2

Safety

You can safely make and use copper pipe structures in your yard and garden. This chapter points out a few of the things you need to do before you get started, while you work, and when you install your structures.

Work Safely

Cutting and assembling copper pipe involves the use of tools and supplies that can be dangerous if used carelessly.

It is up to **you** to read and follow all instructions that come with any tool you use. If you use materials such as flux, solder, and adhesives, **you** must read the instructions and decide if you can use the materials safely.

If you decide to solder copper pipe, the most dangerous tool you use might be a torch. Before using a torch, study all the operating instructions and safety information that comes with the torch. If you don't understand the instructions or don't feel safe using a torch, you can assemble your copper pipe structures with adhesives instead.

Most importantly when using a torch, protect yourself against accidental burns. "Accidental" means you don't know that you are going to burn yourself ahead of time. What you can do ahead of time is protect yourself with gloves, eye protection, and proper clothing.

Next, protect your house and **never** use a torch indoors. Always work outdoors well away from any flammable materials and sources of gasoline vapor including gas cans, lawn mowers, and cars. Have a water hose or fire extinguisher handy.

Use Copper Pipe Structures for Plants Only

Copper pipe trellises, arbors, and other structures can be safely used for their intended purpose of supporting or displaying plants, potted plants, and garden fabrics. And that is all.

Copper pipe structures are **not** intended for:

- jungle gyms or any other children's plaything
- ladders, fences, railings, balusters
- structural supports, steps, stools, chairs
- scaffolding

You get the idea. Use your copper pipe structures for supporting or displaying plants, potted plants, and garden fabrics, and **nothing else**. If you make large trellises or arbors, teach your children not to play on them.

Support your Copper Pipe Structures Properly

A copper pipe trellis or arbor needs to be able to support itself, the plant growing on it, and the force of the wind. You can deal with the first two requirements with the strength of copper pipe itself, and a little bit of common sense — light trellises for light plants, big strong trellises for big heavy vines.

The force of the wind can never be planned for with 100% certainty. In any given year you may hear about or experience winds strong enough to do damage to trees, roofs, and buildings. If winds can blow over a tree, they can certainly blow over any trellis you make. All you can really do is install your structures so they can withstand **normal** weather. Unusually strong winds can damage most anything, and nothing I can tell you in this book will change that.

If you install a trellis or other structure on a nice calm day, it is easy to forget that soon the trellis will be covered with vines and leaves, and that storms and winds will be coming sooner or later. The time to support your trellis is **before** you start using it. Don't put it off until the trellis is covered with plants and there is a storm blowing in.

This book shows ways to support copper pipe structures so they will stay put during **normal** weather. See **"How to Support Copper Pipe Garden Ornaments"** on page 147.

Just remember that even with the best support, an unusually strong wind gust can blow over most anything. Never put your trellises or arbors where they can do damage to anything you care about if they should happen to blow over.

It is possible to grow very massive leafy vines on a trellis, and you may not notice any problem until a very windy day. Don't wait for your trellis to get blown over. Keep all thickly growing vines trimmed so they don't present a solid mass to the wind. Keep some gaps and bare spots so the wind can blow through (and show off your trellis too).

It is a good idea to think about the direction of your prevailing winds, and orient your structures so they don't catch the wind. With an arbor, try to orient the arbor so the wind blows through the archway, not against the sides. With a trellis, install it so the wind blows against the narrow edge, not against the wide face.

CHAPTER 3

Copper Pipe and Fittings

This chapter will introduce you to everything you need to know about copper pipe and the fittings used to assemble the pipe into useful structures.

Types of Copper Pipe

First, understand that copper pipe and fittings are manufactured with **plumbing** applications in mind. Copper pipe and fittings are not expressly manufactured for building trellises or other garden structures. For that reason, the various sizes of pipe and types of fittings are those which are used by plumbers. If plumbers don't need or use a certain size of pipe or a certain type of fitting, then those pipes and fittings are not manufactured.

Don't be put off just because the pipe is normally used for plumbing. Copper plumbing pipe in the US is 99% pure copper, just as durable and attractive as the copper used to make gutters, downspouts, and roofs on high-end homes.

Copper pipe and the common fittings are available in the plumbing department of any home center or hardware store. The home centers normally stock straight copper pipe in ten foot lengths. They also may carry copper pipe in shorter lengths, but at a much higher price per foot. To save money, always buy the ten foot lengths. If transporting a ten foot piece of pipe is a problem, just take your tubing cutter (see page 9) to the store. In the parking lot, you can quickly cut the pipe to a size that will fit in your vehicle.

The home centers normally carry these types of copper pipe:

- ½ inch type "L" and type "M" "hard" pipe, sold as individual straight pieces.
- ¾ inch type "L" and type "M" "hard" pipe, sold as individual straight pieces.
- ¼, ½, and ¾ inch annealed or "soft" pipe, sold as coiled tube, usually in a box.

½ inch hard pipe is the type you will use for building most trellises and small arbors. With good support for the trellis in the ground or against a wall, it is plenty strong enough to hold any type of annual vine and many perennial vines.

¾ inch hard pipe can be used to build large trellises and arbors that will need to hold large perennial vines such as wisteria or trumpet vine.

"Type L" and "Type M" refer to the wall thickness of the pipe. Without going into the details here (See **"Copper Pipe Details and Other Pipe Fittings"** on page 165 if you are interested), "Type L" pipe has greater wall thickness, which makes it more rigid and less prone to denting. Type L is only a little more expensive than type M. Use "type L" when you can.

Be alert when buying pipe – it is easy for the different types of pipe to get mixed up at the home centers as people sort through the selection. Each type of pipe will have its identity printed along the length of the pipe. Each type of pipe also uses a different color for the printing. ½ inch type L pipe will usually have a manufacturer's name and "½ inch type L" printed along the side of the pipe in blue ink. Type M pipe will have its identification printed in red ink.

Soft coiled copper tube can be used to make curved parts of a trellis without using the bending tools required by hard pipe. However, soft tube will always be relatively soft, and can be easily dented or deformed if your trellis is dropped or bumped. Soft tube is also much more expensive than hard (straight) pipe.

For your first few projects, all you need to get is: **ten foot lengths of ½ inch Type L hard copper pipe**.

That may be the only type of pipe you **ever** need to buy. But, after you have bought some pipe and built some projects with this pipe, you can come back to this section with a better understanding of pipe types if you wish.

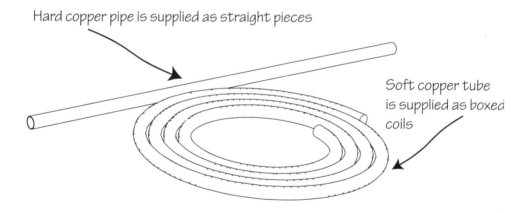

Hard copper pipe is supplied as straight pieces

Soft copper tube is supplied as boxed coils

Cleaning Copper Pipe

After you assemble your projects, you can remove oil, fingerprints, and any flux residue with household cleaners. The best way to remove the manufacturer's ink markings is by rubbing with fine steel wool.

Types of Copper Fittings

When you go to the home center plumbing section, you will find a bewildering array of fittings for copper pipe. The good news is that for building garden structures, you only need to be concerned with six basic fittings. Most other fittings are for specialized plumbing applications and are of no use to the trellis builder.

There are two materials used to make fittings. One is cast brass, the other is wrought copper. Cast brass fittings look like brass, have thick walls, and are heavy. Wrought copper fittings look like copper (very similar to copper pipe itself), have thin walls, and are lighter weight. For building garden structures, get wrought copper fittings.

Pipe fittings are called by the same name as the pipes they fit. A fitting called a ½ inch fitting fits ½ inch pipe. A fitting called a ¾ inch fitting fits a ¾ inch pipe. These sizes are just names, or "nominal sizes", in the same way that a "two by four" piece of lumber does not really measure 2" by 4". Neither the fitting nor the pipe inside or outside diameter is exactly ½ inch or ¾ inch. See **"Copper Pipe Details and Other Pipe Fittings"** on page 165 if you want detailed pipe size information.

Tip	Most of the common fittings are available as individual pieces, and also as "project packs" or "contractor packs" with 10 or 20 pieces in a plastic bag. I suggest you buy the largest pack sizes. Even if you only build a few trellises, you will save money over buying the individual pieces.

Here are the basic fittings you will use, and what they look like:

The 90° Elbow. This fitting is also called a 90° ELL, or just an EL or ELL (since a 90° ELL is the most common type). This fitting allows you to make a right angle corner from two pieces of pipe. There is a less common fitting called a "street Elbow" that you **don't** want.

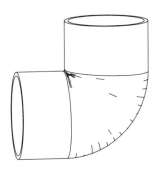

The Tee. This fitting allows you to join a pipe at right angles to two other pipes that are in line with each other. Pipe does not go through a Tee fitting. A Tee fitting accepts three different pipes, one pipe in each opening.

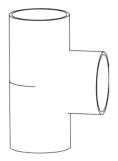

The 45° Elbow. Also called a 45 EL. This fitting allows you to join one pipe to another at a 45° angle (or a 135° angle depending on which way you look at it).

The straight coupling. This fitting allows you to join the end of one length of pipe to the end of another. Pipe does not go through a coupling. A coupling accepts two different pipes.

The end cap. This fitting covers the end of a piece of pipe. For trellis building, it serves to keep rainwater and insects out of your trellises.

The pipe strap. Also called a tube strap. This is not really a fitting, but it is sold in the same area with fittings. It fits around a copper pipe and allows you to fasten copper pipe to another structure such as a fence or the side of a house.

Usually you want fittings that will accept the same size of pipe into each of the openings on the fitting. For instance, you want a ½ inch Elbow to accept ½ inch pipes into each of the ends. This is a normal Elbow. Fittings that accept different sizes are also available. If an Elbow accepts ½ inch pipe at one end and ¾ inch pipe at the other, it is called a ¾ x ½ Reducer Elbow. A Tee that accepts ½ inch pipe on opposite ends, and a ¼ inch pipe from the side is called a ½ x ½ x ¼ Tee.

You don't need to be too concerned about these special sizes. Just be aware that they exist when you shop for fittings, since many times fittings wind up in the wrong bins at the home centers. This is another good reason to buy fittings in "contractor packs". Only the most common fittings (Elbows, Tees, couplings, caps, and straps) are sold in bulk packs, so you can't make a mistake.

THE PIPE AND FITTINGS YOU NEED TO GET STARTED

To make it easy for you on your first trip to buy supplies, here are all the pipe and fittings you need in order to get started on most of the projects in this book:

- One or more ten foot lengths of ½ inch straight "type L" pipe. (Identification printed along the pipe in blue or blue-green ink, and sometimes on the bar code sticker.)
- A bulk pack of ½ inch 90° Elbow fittings and a bulk pack of ½ inch Tee fittings.

If you wish, take along this book on your first trip and you will be able to compare the illustrations of fittings to the actual fittings. And of course you can ask the home center associate that is responsible for the plumbing section to help you get the right items. Remember to take along, or plan to purchase, a tubing cutter if your vehicle can't carry ten foot long pieces of pipe.

CHAPTER 4 *Tools and Supplies for Working with Copper Pipe*

In This Chapter To work with copper pipe, you need tools to cut the pipe. You also need tools and supplies to permanently assemble the cut pipe into the fittings and make a strong garden structure.

Tools for Cutting Pipe

When you think of cutting metal, a hacksaw might be the first tool that comes to mind. But instead of a hacksaw, I strongly recommend you use a tool known as a **Tubing Cutter** to cut copper pipe.

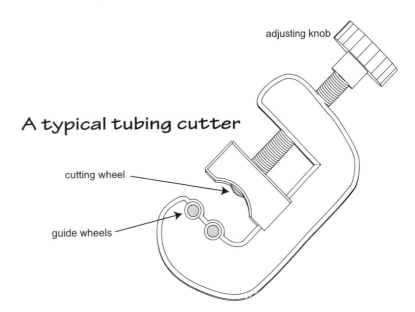

adjusting knob

A typical tubing cutter

cutting wheel

guide wheels

A good tubing cutter is about the same cost as a good quality hacksaw, but it has these advantages over a hacksaw:

- You do not need to clamp the pipe or hold it in a vise. You do not need a workbench or a table.

- A tubing cutter does not make metal chips or dust, so it does not waste pipe.

- A tubing cutter will cut exactly at your mark, without wandering.
- A tubing cutter always cuts square.
- A tubing cutter never chatters or gets stuck in the cut.
- A tubing cutter does not leave metal burs that need to be cleaned off the outside of the pipe.
- A tubing cutter is practically effortless to use.
- A tubing cutter is smaller and more portable than a hacksaw. You can easily take it with you when buying pipe and cut the pipe to a size that will fit in your vehicle.

Are those enough advantages for you? If not, go ahead and use your old hacksaw on your first project. Then when you want to make some more projects, invest in a tubing cutter, and you will truly appreciate using it!

Tubing cutters usually come with instructions. But here are the steps in case you want a review:

1. Put the pipe in the tubing cutter and tighten the knob until the cutting wheel is firmly against your cutting mark.
2. Hold the pipe still, and rotate the tubing cutter around the pipe in the direction shown, for one complete revolution.
3. The cutter wheel will make a slight groove in the pipe, and will no longer be tight against the pipe. Tighten the knob until the cutter wheel is tight against the pipe again.
4. Repeat steps 2 and 3 until the pipe is cut through, which should be several revolutions with tightening between each revolution. If it takes longer on your first attempts, next time just tighten the knob a little more firmly than you have been after each revolution.

After you get some experience, you will notice that you can turn the adjusting knob at the same time you are rotating the cutter around the pipe, and you will be able to cut pipe much faster.

To use a tubing cutter, hold the pipe still and rotate the tubing cutter around the pipe in the direction shown. Turn the adjusting knob to keep the cutting wheel in contact with the pipe.

Tools for Assembling

I suggest you solder your copper pipe projects if at all possible. However, it is possible to use epoxy or other adhesives to assemble your projects. If you really don't want to solder, then you don't need a torch, but you still need tools for reaming and cleaning the pipe.

Here is why I suggest soldering:

- With practice, your joints will be stronger and more watertight. Copper pipe soldered to a fitting is just as strong as or stronger than the pipe itself.

- Soldered joints become rigid as soon as the solder cools, and you can then go on to your next joint without waiting more than a minute or so. All types of adhesives take at least several minutes to set, which not only slows you down but makes it much more likely that parts will shift out of alignment during the set-up period.

- When soldering, you can assemble a project in a jig or with hose clamps (more on that later) and solder the joints without taking anything apart. When using adhesives, you might have to do a "dry fit" to make sure everything fits correctly, then take everything apart, put adhesive on each joint, and reassemble.

- If you make a mistake, soldered joints can be re-heated and taken apart. After some types of adhesive joints set up, you cannot take the joint apart.

There are some drawbacks to soldering, but I do not think they outweigh the advantages, especially if you will be making several projects or even one large project:

- Soldering requires tools and supplies you may not need for anything else.

- Soldering may require some practice (maybe 10 joints!) to get good at it.

- Soldering involves high heat and open flame, which therefore requires safety precautions in order to protect yourself and your work area. For personal safety, wear gloves, eye protection, and the proper clothing. For fire safety, soldering **must** be done outdoors. **Never** use a torch indoors.

So, assuming that you will be soldering, here is the tool you need:

A PROPANE OR **MAPP** GAS TORCH

You may have used a basic propane torch, or seen a basic propane torch being used. This type of torch consists of a propane tank, and a torch head which screws to the tank. To light this type of torch, you must turn a knob on the torch head, which starts the flow of gas from the tank. Then you must use a "sparker" to ignite the gas, and finally adjust the flow of gas to adjust the flame. To turn it off, you must turn the knob to stop the flow of gas.

There are significant safety concerns with these old torches. It is possible to set the torch down, but leave the flame on. A moment of inattention could lead to a tipped-over, yet still burning torch. It is also possible to have the flame go out, but the gas still be turned on, which could lead to a dangerous "flash" if you try to re-light the torch too soon.

In the past few years, there has been a great development in the world of torches, namely "self-igniting" torches. These newer torches still use a tank of gas and a torch head, but the torch head is special. All you have to do is hold the torch in one hand, and press a button. This starts the flow of gas, ignites the gas, and adjusts the flame. Releasing the button turns the torch off completely.

Safety! Self-igniting torches are generally much safer than older torches. If you are not holding the torch with the button depressed, the flame goes out and the flow of gas is turned off. However, there is one thing to be extremely careful about, and that is to never point the torch at any part of your body, whether the torch is on or off. Because the torch is so easy to ignite, you could burn yourself the moment you press the ignite button if the torch is pointed in the wrong direction.

In practical terms, the advantage of a self-igniting torch is that when you want to solder a joint, you just pick up the torch, push the button, and go to work. When finished with the joint, just set the torch down. If you are making a project with lots of joints, this speed and convenience is significant. If you don't already have a torch, I suggest getting a self igniting type as your first torch, if it is within your budget. They are somewhat more expensive than basic torches.

A typical self-igniting torch

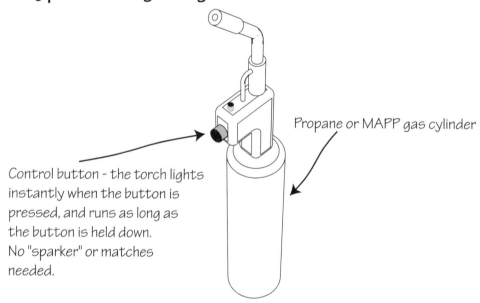

Control button - the torch lights instantly when the button is pressed, and runs as long as the button is held down. No "sparker" or matches needed.

Propane or MAPP gas cylinder

You can get torches designed for one or both of two types of fuel. Basic torches are usually designed to use only propane gas or only MAPP gas. Most self-igniting torches can use either type of gas.

The practical difference between MAPP gas and propane gas is that MAPP gas burns hotter than propane gas. This means you can heat a joint more quickly, and therefore work faster.

You can start with propane gas if you get a self igniting torch. After you use up your first tank of propane gas, you can decide for yourself whether you care enough about working faster to buy the more expensive MAPP gas.

Supplies for Soldering

In addition to a torch, you need three other things:

- Tools or materials to clean the copper pipe and fittings
- Flux
- Solder.

TOOLS OR MATERIALS TO CLEAN PIPES AND FITTINGS

If you cut copper pipe with a hacksaw, there will be burs on the pipe that will prevent a fitting from going over the pipe. You can use plumber's sand cloth, a file, or a special plumber's "reamer" tool to remove the burs. The reamer tool is the fastest method.

Copper pipe and fittings must be cleaned to expose fresh new copper, before applying flux or adhesive. You can use plumber's sand cloth, which is a type of emery cloth, or a special "wire brush" tool made for the purpose. Start with sand cloth. If you find you are interested in making more than a few copper pipe garden structures, then you will find the "wire brush" type pipe cleaner very fast and easy.

reamer tool

wire brush
pipe cleaning
tools

Plumber's sand cloth and the special wire brush pipe cleaning tools are usually available in the plumbing department of any home center or hardware store, near the flux and solder.

FLUX

Flux is special material with the consistency of petroleum jelly. It is applied with a small brush to the outside of the copper pipe and the inside of the copper fitting, before you assemble the joint for soldering.

The basic purpose of flux is to help solder stick permanently to both the copper pipe and the copper fitting.

With flux and solder, you get a strong, permanent joint. Without flux you may have solder that doesn't stick to either the pipe or fitting or both, and a joint that may crack, allow water to get in, or separate completely. So, use flux!

SOLDER

Solder is a relatively low-melting point metal or combination of metals that will stick very strongly to copper pipe and fittings and make permanent joints (as long as you use flux first!). The way solder is normally sold, it looks like thick gray wire, wound around a spool.

Until recently, most solder was made of lead and tin. Lead solder is still available, but because of health concerns about using lead where it may come into contact with drinking water, most solders now use tin in combination with other metals.

When you go to buy solder and flux, you will find a confusing array of different types, brands, and package sizes. Plumbers may need all those types for different purposes, but us trellis builders don't! Some manufacturers have realized that not all their customers are professional plumbers, so they have packaged some kits for a homeowner's convenience. These kits are available at most home centers, in or near the area that has solder and flux separately.

Some of these kits are just solder, flux, and a small brush to apply the flux. Other kits offer everything you need – solder, flux, brush, sand cloth, a torch, and an instruction booklet.

I suggest you get a prepackaged solder and flux kit to start with. After you have worked with one combination of solder and flux, and it works for you, you can buy larger packages of the same type and brand solder and flux for your later projects, and save a little money. If you need a torch anyway, consider getting one of the kits that includes a torch.

The kits usually have "non-lead" type solder. Read the solder ingredients on the package just to be sure. My experience is that non-lead solders are plenty strong and easy to work with, so there is no reason to use a solder containing lead.

Plumber's sand cloth

Solder

Flux and brushes

Tools and Supplies You Need to Get Started

If you will be assembling with adhesives, you need:

- A tubing cutter.
- Plumber's sand cloth a or wire brush cleaning tool.
- Adhesives (see page 23).

If you will be assembling with solder, you need:

- A tubing cutter.
- A propane or MAPP gas torch.
- Plumber's sand cloth or a wire brush cleaning tool.
- Flux
- Solder
- Or a prepackaged kit that has some or most of the above.

CHAPTER 5

How to Solder Copper Pipe

In This Chapter

Soldering copper pipe lets you make fast, strong, watertight, permanent connections for your copper projects.

Soldering is the best, but not the only way you can assemble your projects. If you don't wish to solder, skip this chapter and read the next chapter on using adhesives.

About Soldering

The best way for you to join copper pipe permanently is by using fittings and soldering. This is the same method plumbers use to make strong, watertight plumbing connections. Soldering copper pipe is sometimes called "sweating" pipe or "making sweat connections", as opposed to other plumbing connections that use threads or compression fittings.

SOLDERING VERSUS BRAZING AND WELDING

There are several standard ways to join metals such as copper. Among them are soldering, brazing, and welding. Soldering is the simplest method, and the only method shown in this book. If you don't care about the details, but just want to know how to do it, you can skip to the next section now.

Soldering copper pipe is the process of using molten solder to fill the tiny gap between a copper pipe and a fitting. The solder bonds to both the copper pipe and the fitting to make a strong watertight joint. Soldering uses temperatures ranging from 350° F to 600° F.

You **must** use fittings to solder copper pipe. You cannot just assemble copper pipe, with or without miter joints or other types of joinery, and expect solder to hold the pieces together like glue. Solder relies on the parts being in very close contact, with a large surface area over which the solder can bond. Fittings provide both these requirements.

Solder does **not** melt into or become part of copper. Soldering is **not** a process of melting the copper pipe or fitting. (The copper alloy used for plumbing pipe melts at about 1981° F.)

Brazing is a process of causing a metal "brazing rod", usually coated with flux, to melt into the joint between copper pipe and a fitting. Brazing takes place at temperatures between 1100° F and 1500° F. Brazing makes a stronger joint than soldering because the filler metal in brazing rods is a stronger metal than that used for soldering. However, the extra strength of brazing is not significant for making garden structures, or most plumbing applications either. Brazing is sometimes called "silver soldering" or "hard soldering" because the brazing rod filler metal can contain silver or other metals which melt at much higher temperatures than tin-based solder.

Welding is a process of actually melting the metal in two pieces of copper in close contact. When this molten metal has cooled, the two pieces are effectively one piece.

Brazing and welding require specialized equipment and training, and are not really suitable techniques for the average gardener who just wants to do some projects for his or her yard. Neither brazing nor welding is covered in this book. All the projects in this book are done with fittings and soldering, or you can use fittings and adhesives if you wish.

If you should decide that you like making copper garden structures so much that you want to do it for a living, then you can learn about brazing and welding, and make designs not limited to what copper plumbing fittings can do. But first, start with soldering!

Soldering Procedure

To solder copper pipe, you need to do just four things:

1. Clean the pipe and fitting.
2. Flux the pipe and fitting.
3. Assemble the pipe and fitting tightly and squarely.
4. Heat the joint and cause solder to flow into the joint.

CLEANING COPPER PIPE AND FITTINGS

The copper pipe and fittings you buy at the store have already started to oxidize from exposure to oxygen in the air. Their surfaces are not fresh, bare copper, but have a very thin layer of this oxidation covering the copper. You need to remove this oxidation so that the flux and the solder can both work on fresh, bare copper.

All you need to do is use some plumber's sand cloth or a special wire brush tool (see page 13) and rub away the oxidation until you see bright shiny copper.

Do this to the outside end of the copper pipe that goes into your fitting, and the inside of the fitting itself. Use a dry rag to wipe off any dust that may be on the fitting after you clean it.

FLUXING COPPER PIPE AND FITTINGS

Once your pipe and fittings are clean, use a small brush called an "acid brush" (usually included with kits of flux and solder) and coat the bright clean copper with flux. You don't need gobs of flux; a thin coat is all that is necessary. The flux looks very much like petroleum jelly – just make sure the copper looks greasy, with no bare spots.

Do this to the outside end of the copper pipe, and the inside of the fitting – the same parts you cleaned.

ASSEMBLING THE PIPE AND FITTING

Copper fittings are designed to allow copper pipe to enter about 3/8" into the fitting, and no more. Assemble the pipe into the fitting by pressing it in until it stops, then turn the fitting or the pipe back and forth a little to spread the flux evenly.

Make sure your fitting is facing the right way. A Tee fitting can be assembled so that the right angle faces to the inside of a trellis or the outside of a trellis, or anywhere in between. If you are following one of the projects in this book, just check the illustrations to be sure you have it right.

On many projects, you can clean, flux, and assemble the whole project before doing any soldering. This will insure that all the fittings are in the right places and facing the right way.

On other projects, you can use jigs to hold the pieces in correct alignment while soldering, or use hose clamps to hold pieces in alignment. See **"Measuring Jigs, Assembly Jigs, and Clamping"** on page 27 for more information.

SAFETY BEFORE SOLDERING

Now you are almost ready to do the actual soldering. But before you start, take steps to ensure your safety. If you don't feel safe using a torch, then assemble your projects with adhesives instead– see the next chapter.

Safety!

- Always wear leather gloves, long sleeve shirts, long pants, shoes, and protective eye wear. Molten solder can drip and splash. Protect yourself **before** you start soldering, most especially your eyes, hands, arms, and feet. Gloves are a necessity. In addition to getting hit by molten solder, there is always the possibility that you will absent-mindedly touch a pipe or a joint that is still hot enough to burn. Gloves are your only protection – get some that cover your wrists and overlap the sleeves of a long sleeve shirt.

- Always solder with the workpiece below or in front of you, such as on a table or sawhorse. Never solder over your head, or crawl under something to solder it. That is a sure way to have molten solder drip on your face or down your shirt. Never climb ladders when using a torch, or use a torch anywhere except with both feet on the ground.

- Always make sure your torch is pointed away from your body. If working outdoors in bright light, sometimes the flame can be hard to see. Never check for a flame by holding your hand in front of a torch! Use a long piece of solder if you must. Better, move to a shaded spot where you can see the flame.

- **Always work outdoors** in a clean, uncluttered space. Use your common sense and don't use a torch near sources of gasoline vapor – cars, lawnmowers, gas cans etc.

- Always have a garden hose or fire extinguisher handy.

SOLDERING TECHNIQUE

1. Clean the inside of the fitting and the outside of the copper pipe. Flux the pipe, and insert the pipe into the fitting. Support the pipe in any way necessary so that you **do not** need to hold it or touch it. The pipe is going to get hot enough to burn you, even a foot or more away from where you direct the torch.

2. Solder and flux may both drip. Protect your lawn or deck or whatever surface you are working on. Some damp cardboard works fine.

3. Put on gloves and eye protection. Have your torch and a dry rag handy. Uncoil several inches of solder from the spool so you can keep your hand well away from the torch flame.

4. Start the torch and direct the flame at the end of the pipe near the joint. The torch head should be about 2" away from the pipe. After briefly heating the pipe, start moving the flame slowly back and forth between the end of the pipe and the fitting. Depending on the lighting conditions, you may not be able to see the flame itself. But if you pay attention to the fitting you will see the copper change colors as it gets hot, and the flux will liquefy.

5. After about 5 seconds of heating, you should see some flux starting to bubble. Move the flame to the center of the fitting, away from the joint, and heat about 5 seconds longer. Touch the tip of the solder to the joint between the pipe and fitting, away from the flame.

Note	Never put the flame directly on the solder or the solder in the flame. Always heat the pipe and fitting only, and they will melt the solder.

6. If the solder starts to melt, feed the solder directly into the joint at that one spot.

7. If the solder does not start to melt, remove the solder, heat the fitting a little more, and then try again until the solder starts to melt and you can feed it into the joint.

8. When the solder starts to flow into the joint, watch the joint. The heated fitting and pipe should cause the solder to melt and flow into the entire joint. You do not need to move the solder all around the joint.

9. As soon as you see solder flow all around the joint, remove the flame and let the joint cool. If you are working above a joint, you won't be able to see the bottom of the joint of course, and you should **not** try to see the bottom of the joint. Just assume that when you see solder fill in the top of the joint, that it has also filled in the bottom of the joint.

10. If you used too much solder and there is a big drip, you can use the dry rag to wipe it off. However, this will make a permanent tin-colored smear of solder on the pipe. Instead, you can try touching the dry rag to the drip of solder and wicking the drip onto the rag. You can also try touching the tip of the soldering wire to the drip. Both of these techniques require that you catch the drip just before it cools and solidifies, and they take some practice. Don't worry too much about drips. They will hardly be noticeable after the copper has been outdoors for awhile. Plus, your soldering technique will improve so this won't happen too often.

SOLUTIONS TO COMMON SOLDERING PROBLEMS

Everything happens too quickly.

- This is a common feeling when first starting to solder. With just a little bit of practice (10 joints or so) you will probably get the hang of it and be able to better control each step of the process. Until then, just do the best you can. Almost any amount of solder will hold a joint together, whether it is technically not enough or way too much. If you start with a simple project like a pot trellis, the exact amount of solder in the joint is of no real concern— the parts of the project will be permanently fastened no matter how bad the joint looks.

- You may be too concerned about getting good results. If this is the case, sacrifice some pipe and some fittings and just practice soldering, without any concern about whether you are making something usable.

- A useful learning technique is to read the instructions, solder a joint, and re-read the instructions. You will probably notice something you missed or something that you didn't understand just from reading. Solder another joint with your new knowledge, re-read the instructions and so on. Don't be too concerned about making mistakes.

Solder does not fill the joint.

- You may not have used enough solder. Before soldering ½ inch pipe, try this: make a bend in the solder wire about ½ inch from the end. While soldering, feed solder into the joint up to the bend. You can adjust the position of the bend on the solder for your next joint if the joint still does not fill, or if you used too much. For ¾ inch pipe, allow about ¾ inch of solder.

- The joint may not have been hot enough. You will know this because it will be difficult to get the solder to flow. Feeding solder into a properly heated joint is effortless, so heat the joint longer before feeding the solder into the joint.

- The joint may have been too hot and burned away some of the flux. Flux helps the solder flow into the joint. It is normal for the flux to liquefy and start bubbling, but it should not smoke or turn black. You are heating the joint too long or you have the torch too close to the joint if the flux burns away.

Too much solder in the joint, causing drips. Use the same technique of bending the solder wire to indicate how much to use, as mentioned previously. This will help you to consistently put the right amount of solder in all your joints.

The flux burns away. Bubbling flux is normal. But if you heat a joint and notice the flux smoking and turning black, stop. Let the joint cool, re-clean the joint and re-flux the joint before continuing. Without flux in the joint you can't make a good joint. If you burn flux all the time, it means you are holding the flame too close to the joint, or holding the flame in one place too long. Back off the flame a bit and keep the flame slowly moving between the pipe and fitting so no one spot gets overheated. Touch the solder to the joint sooner to see if the joint is hot enough, and feed the solder into the joint as soon as the joint can melt the solder.

HOW TO DE-SOLDER

Sooner or later you will assemble a fitting facing the wrong direction. Here is how to de-solder, assuming you caught the mistake in time and did not solder other pipes into the same fitting:

1. Support the pipe that has the fitting to be de-soldered in a vise or other clamp. You will need to pull on the fitting, and you do not want to have to touch the pipe to keep it steady. The pipe is going to get very hot again.

2. You can de-solder a fitting by using the same heating technique you used to solder it. When you see the solder in the joint melt, move the flame to the opposite end of the fitting and use a pair of pliers to twist and pull on the fitting.

3. The fitting should come off. The fitting won't be usable again. The pipe will have a coating of solder that will interfere with putting a new fitting on. While the pipe is still hot, carefully use a dry rag to remove as much solder as possible from the pipe.

4. After the pipe cools you can clean it to bare copper with sand cloth and attach another fitting as usual.

CHAPTER 6 *How to Use Adhesives*

You can use adhesives to assemble some copper pipe projects if you prefer not to solder. Here's how.

Before you Use Adhesive

No adhesive is as strong or durable as solder.

- Adhesives may break or crack if put under too much strain.
- Adhesives may fail after some period of exposure to direct sunlight, freezing temperatures, water, garden chemicals, or pollution.

Here are some guidelines:

- Use solder on all projects if at all possible.
- If you must use adhesives, they are suitable for simple projects and smaller size trellises that will have good support from concrete, "T" posts in the ground, or will be fastened to a wall or other support.
- For larger free standing structures or arbors, use solder. The weight of a large vine combined with the force of wind blowing on the vine could easily cause an adhesive joint to crack or pull apart.
- All adhesives **must** be used with fittings. You cannot simply glue pieces of pipe to each other and expect good results.
- copper pipe must be cleaned before using adhesive. See **"Cleaning copper pipe and fittings"** on page 18.

Types of Adhesives for Copper Pipe

There are two main types of adhesives you can use with acceptable results on copper pipe. One is epoxy, the other is construction adhesive.

Select the type of adhesive to use with your projects by consulting the following information:

Adhesive Type	Cost	Initial Set or "Open" Time	Complete Cure Time	Can disassemble joint?
Special Copper Bonding Epoxy	More expensive	5 minutes	20 minutes	Yes, with heat from torch
Construction Adhesive	Less expensive	10 minutes	24 hours	Yes, with force

Epoxy for Copper Pipe

There are special epoxies formulated for use with copper pipe and fittings. These epoxies are available in the plumbing section of most home centers, in the same area as flux and solder. The epoxy is supplied as two thick liquid components in a double-barreled plunger so you can dispense equal amounts of the two components. There are other epoxies sold in the plumbing section that are supplied as sticks of putty or clay consistency material that you mix in your hands. That type of epoxy is not used for assembling fittings.

The special copper bonding epoxy comes with complete instructions for use with copper pipe and fittings, so there is no need to repeat the basic instructions here. I will mention some specific tips not covered in the instructions:

- The epoxy comes with a storage cap attached between the two plungers. Remove this and save it so you can keep the epoxy fresh between uses. Before squeezing any epoxy, cut off the ends of the tubes at the groove near the tip and test fit the storage cap. You may need to ream out the holes in the nozzles a little so the storage cap will fit, and it is easier to do it before the epoxy gums up the nozzles.

- You will get epoxy all over your hands while assembling pipe, so wear disposable gloves. You can get cheap vinyl disposable gloves in the paint section of the home centers, or at a drugstore. You will get epoxy on your work table, so protect it with plastic sheet or newspaper. This will also keep your trellis projects from getting accidentally glued to the table.

- Always have all your parts cut, cleaned, and dry fit before mixing epoxy. There is no time to do any of this after you mix the epoxy. Epoxy starts to set up quickly. On your first project, only mix and use enough epoxy to make a couple of joints, about a half teaspoon. After you get some experience, you will know how many joints you can do before the epoxy starts to set.

- Don't try to do too much at one time. Assemble fittings to both ends of a single pipe for instance, and let that epoxy cure. Then assemble other parts to that part. If you try to do too much at once it can be extremely frustrating, with gooey parts slipping out of one fitting while you try to put together the next, or joints you thought were aligned properly rotating and warping. Make as many small assemblies as you can, wait for the epoxy to cure, and then assemble those parts to each other.

- As you assemble pipe and fittings with epoxy, a lot of excess epoxy will squeeze out of the joint. Wipe around the joint with a wooden craft stick to remove the excess, and use the excess on the next joint.

One thing to be very careful about is to correctly orient the pipe in the fitting when you assemble the two parts. Get in the habit of dry fitting the parts together and making marks on the pipe and the fitting that show the correct alignment of the pipe in the fitting.

The most important thing to know about using this epoxy is that it sets quickly. This can be an advantage if you are assembling a project with a jig because you can start working on the next section reasonably quickly. It can be a disaster if you try to assemble a large project and the epoxy starts to set before you have everything in alignment.

There are many other brands and types of epoxy sold as adhesives. They may or may not work well to permanently fasten copper pipe. Try to use the type specifically formulated for copper pipe instead of gambling on other types that may not perform as well.

Construction Adhesive for Copper Pipe

In my tests (see the end of this chapter) construction adhesive was not nearly as strong as the copper bonding epoxy. I suggest using construction adhesive only on pot trellises, or small size trellises that will be supported mostly by a fence or wall. Any kind of twisting force, such as from the wind blowing against a free-standing trellis, could cause the joints to fail.

All construction adhesive comes with general instructions right on the tube of adhesive, but here are some more specific instructions for working with copper pipe:

1. Clean the end of the pipe and the inside of the fitting with sand cloth or a wire brush cleaning tool.
2. Dry fit the pipe and fitting together. If necessary, make marks on the pipe and the fitting that show the correct orientation of the pipe in the fitting.
3. Put a small amount of construction adhesive all around the end of the pipe.
4. Insert the pipe in the fitting and twist it back and forth to distribute the adhesive.
5. Remove the pipe from the fitting and allow a few seconds for the adhesive to get tacky.
6. Reassemble the pipe in the fitting permanently and wipe off any excess adhesive. Be sure the fitting is oriented in the correct direction — after a few minutes you may not be able to turn the fitting without breaking the bond.

Read the tips under the epoxy section also. In particular, make small assemblies of parts, let them cure completely, and then assemble more parts to the cured parts.

Construction adhesives have a slightly longer "open" time than epoxy. This is an advantage if you are assembling a larger project because you will have a little more time to assemble the parts and make adjustments.

Construction adhesives require a much longer final curing time than epoxy. Even if the construction adhesive claims that it "sets completely in one hour" or something like that, for maximum strength don't disturb your project for about 24 hours after assembly.

Adhesives Tested

I tested the following adhesives on copper pipe and fittings and got the results noted. For my tests, I used the various adhesives to attach two fittings to a short length of pipe. After the curing period recommended by the manufacturer, I used two 18" long pipes in the fittings as levers, and attempted to twist the fittings off the pipe with muscle power only.

Copper Bonding Epoxy

After a complete cure I used the levers to apply force to the fittings, to the point that the lever pipes almost bent. One glue joint failed and allowed the fitting to rotate around the pipe with difficulty, but the fitting could not be removed by hand. Epoxy had seeped into the fitting and the end of the pipe and formed a hard plug in the fitting which kept the pipe attached.

Top Brand Exterior Grade Construction Adhesive

After a complete cure, I was able to break the glued joint with moderate force on the levers. The fitting stayed connected to the pipe however, and could not be removed by hand.

Polyurethane Glue

This glue was a well known brand. The package said the glue could be used to fasten metal. After following all directions, which included cleaning the pipes and dampening the metal, I applied the glue and let it cure for 24 hours. In testing, the glue resisted fairly heavy force from the levers, but then a joint failed completely and I was able to remove the fitting from the pipe by hand. This glue may be acceptable for making pot trellises, wall medallions, fastening the end caps on poles, and other low-stress uses.

Super Glue

This was a gel type super glue that claimed it would fasten metal. After a complete cure, the fitting twisted off the pipe fairly easily with the use of levers, and I was able to remove the fitting from the pipe by hand.

100% Silicone Caulk

This caulk was a top brand, and claimed to have excellent adhesion to metal. I thoroughly cleaned a pipe and fitting, applied as much caulk as could possibly go between them (which wasn't much), and let the caulk cure completely. I was able to twist the fitting off by hand without using any levers.

Plastic Glue

This is another general purpose adhesive that I have used with excellent results on plastic. The package claimed that it also worked well on metal. My testing showed it was even worse than the silicone.

Hot Melt Glue

Hot Melt Glue was ineffective on copper pipe. The copper pipe conducted heat so readily that the hot melt glue almost instantly hardened and I couldn't even assemble a fitting. I also put hot melt glue on top of copper pipe just to see if it would stick, but the cooled glue peeled right off.

CHAPTER 7 *Measuring Jigs, Assembly Jigs, and Clamping*

In This Chapter	Use a jig to accurately measure pipe for cutting. Use jigs and clamps to hold your trellis projects together while testing the fit or doing the final assembly.

A Hacksaw Measuring and Cutting Jig

Note	A jig is any device that helps you accomplish a repetitive task more easily and do the task with greater accuracy.

If you use a hacksaw to cut pipe, the following illustration shows a simple setup that lets you cut consistent lengths easily.

How to get good results if you use a hacksaw

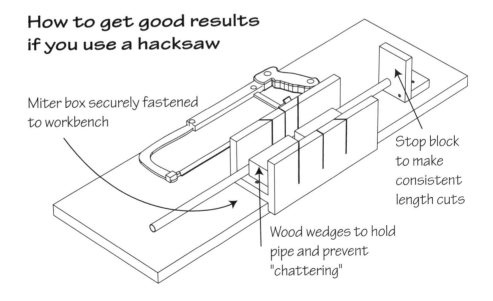

Miter box securely fastened to workbench

Stop block to make consistent length cuts

Wood wedges to hold pipe and prevent "chattering"

Why Use a Measuring Jig?

When building a trellis, you will typically have a dozen or more pieces of pipe to cut to the same length. Of course you can use a tape measure to mark for each cut. But using a tape measure to mark pipe can get pretty tedious and it is easy to mark 11-3/16" or 11-5/16" when what you really wanted was exactly 11-1/4". Small errors in each pipe length can add up to a noticeable error when you put all the pipes together to make a trellis.

Instead of measuring and marking each cut, you can use a jig that allows you to mark the identical cut over and over, without measuring.

How to Make a Measuring Jig

Measuring jig made from wood

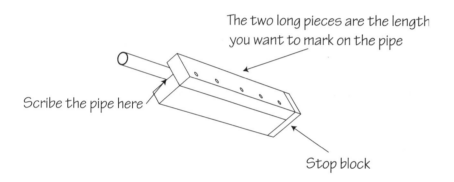

The two long pieces are the length you want to mark on the pipe

Scribe the pipe here

Stop block

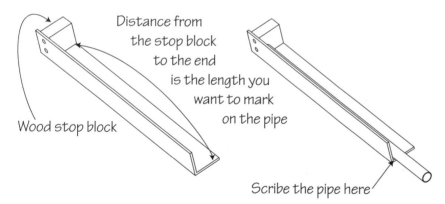

Distance from the stop block to the end is the length you want to mark on the pipe

Wood stop block

Scribe the pipe here

Measuring jig made from aluminum angle

This style of jig is completely portable and easy to use. You can make the jig from wood or aluminum angle, whichever is easier for you to cut and fasten.

For a wooden jig, you can use 1x2 lumber.

Constructing the jig should be self explanatory from looking at the illustrations. The stop block is exactly the same distance from the marking end of the jig as the length of pipe you want to cut.

HOW TO USE THE MEASURING JIG

1. Put the jig over a length of pipe that you want to mark. The end of the pipe goes against the stop block.

2. Mark the pipe at the other end of the jig. A scratch awl or carbide tipped scriber will make the most accurate mark.

3. Use your tubing cutter to cut the pipe at the mark by putting the cutter wheel directly on the scribed mark.

Why Use Assembly Jigs?

To make a trellis project you cut all your pipe to the correct sizes and assemble the pipe into fittings. But how do you know that the trellis will come out square and straight? How do you know all the pipe is fully seated in the fittings?

You can "eyeball" each piece as you assemble the structure to try to make it look right. But some small errors can creep in, especially when assembling a lot of parts. Pipe has a small amount of "wiggle room" in a fitting and you can easily assemble the pipe with a small tilt to one side or another. Small errors repeated over and over in each section of a tall trellis can result in a finished trellis that leans to one side, twists, or weaves back and forth.

Instead of the eyeball method of assembling your projects, you can use simple jigs as assembly aids and get much better results.

Table Top Assembly

The simplest aid for accurately assembling a flat trellis begins with a large flat surface. A large, flat table or workbench on a level floor is ideal. You can also work on a flat, level garage floor or other concrete slab. Sawhorses with a plywood top, set on a level surface such as a deck would also suit the purpose. Just make sure your surface is flat and level. Any warp in a piece of plywood used as a table top will be duplicated in a trellis you build on that table, for instance.

The flat surface by itself is enough if you are assembling with adhesive. Just make sure you don't glue the fittings to the surface by accident.

The flat surface is not enough if you are assembling with solder. All your trellis pipe and fittings would rest on the surface and interfere with soldering.

Table top assembly

Table must be flat and 2x4s must be free of warps. Use hardboard over the table top if you want to protect the table from scorching during soldering.

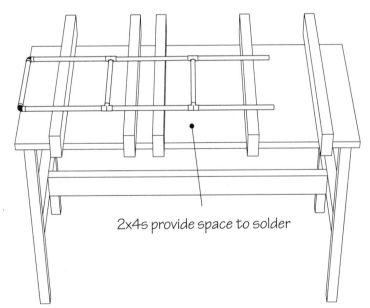

2x4s provide space to solder

Instead, use pieces of 2x4 lumber as supports between the table and the trellis you are assembling. The pieces of lumber should also be free of warps, twists, or bows, and must be all the same dimension.

With a flat level surface and some good 2x4 lumber, you can assemble any flat trellis as shown in the illustration. The pipes of the trellis are supported by the 2x4s, leaving the fittings free to solder.

Since the level surface should result in a flat trellis, all you need to check before final assembly is that all the pipe is fully seated in the fittings. Measure across the width of the trellis at several points, and measure from top to bottom at each end. Any measurements different by more than 1/8 inch or so mean that something is out of alignment - either some pipe is cut to the wrong size, or some pipe is not fully seated in the fittings.

If you are making a typical trellis that should be a rectangle, you can take diagonal measurements from each corner as shown. If your trellis is a true rectangle the measurements will be the same. If the measurements are different, make whatever adjustments you need to correct the problem.

Checking a trellis for square before final assembly

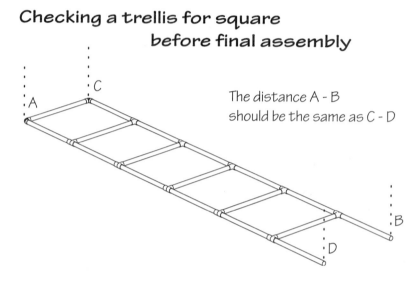

The distance A - B should be the same as C - D

A Jig for a Repetitive Trellis Pattern

Many trellises and arbor uprights use a repetitive rectangular arrangement of cross bars and vertical bars. You can easily make a jig for building this type of trellis accurately. The jig will allow you to build a trellis of any length, not limited to the size of your table or workbench. You can support the jig between two sawhorses and eliminate the need for a table or workbench altogether.

The jig provides a way to hold two rectangular trellis sections in perfect alignment with each other. As you finish each section you move the trellis along the jig and work on the next section.

This jig is intended for use with soldered joints because soldered joints are strong as soon as the solder cools. You could use this jig for assembling with adhesive, but you would have to wait while the adhesive cured completely before doing the next section of the trellis.

BEFORE YOU MAKE THIS JIG

This jig holds pipe in alignment by holding the outside of the pipes. But the dimensions given with the projects in this book are for **center to center** distances. If you want the center to center dimensions of the pipe in your trellis sections to be a certain size, you must make the jig fit the outside of the pipe when the correct size pipe is assembled in fittings.

For instance, if you are using ½ inch diameter pipe and you want a center to center distance between pipes in your trellis of 12", you would cut the pipes to 11-1/4" to allow for the space taken up by fittings. Then you make the jig fit the outside of those assembled pipes and fittings. More information on dimensions and measuring is given on page 35.

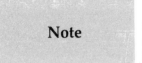

Note   Make the cuts in the pipe with the same cutting tool you will be using to cut all the parts of the trellis. If you cut on a mark with a hacksaw, the cut pipe will be a slightly different length than if you cut on the same mark with a tubing cutter, because a hacksaw makes a kerf (it removes metal).

How to Make This Jig

Assembly jig during construction

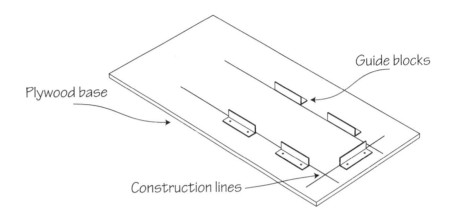

1. Cut pipe for two sections of the trellis you will be building, and assemble the two sections with Tee connectors, but don't solder or use adhesive. Set the trellis sections aside for later

2. You need a piece of ¾ inch thick plywood that has a width about twice your trellis width and about three times the length of a single trellis section. Get an absolutely flat piece of plywood for the jig. Any warp in the plywood will be duplicated in the trellises you make in the jig.

3. Get some 1x2 lumber to use as the alignment guides on the jig. An alternative is to use aluminum angle, as shown in the illustrations.

4. Draw parallel lines down the length of the jig that represent the width of the trellis you will be building. You can measure this distance from the section you made in step 1. For instance, if the width of your trellis will be 12-5/8", measured from **outside to outside** of the pipes, make the lines 12-5/8" apart.

5. Draw a line 6" from one end of the jig, perpendicular to the parallel lines.

6. Cut five 1x2 blocks or aluminum angle to about 4" long. Fasten one block at the midpoint of the line from step 5. Fasten the other four blocks, with their edges along the lines, at two places on each side of the jig. To determine the spacing, place the two trellis sections you make in step 1 on the plywood, between the lines. Space the blocks so they will be about at the midpoint of a trellis section. You don't want the blocks to interfere with the fittings.

7. Put your two trellis sections in the jig, make sure the three cross bars are parallel, and fasten the remaining block guides to the plywood as shown in the next illustration. All blocks should be very snug against the pipe —no "wiggle room". With all blocks in place, you should not be able to move the trellis sections or pipes in any direction except up.

8. Test that the block guides are accurate by removing your trellis sections, turning them end for end, and replacing in the jig. The sections should be just as snug either way.

9. At the places shown, cut holes through the plywood. The holes are so you can solder the joints in those two spots without setting fire to the plywood. You can make the holes with a jigsaw, coping saw or hole saw.

HOW TO USE THE JIG

1. Cut the pipe you need to make two sections of the trellis. Clean and flux the pipe and fittings and assemble the sections.

2. Put both sections in the jig.

3. Solder all the joints in each fitting over the holes in the jig.

4. As soon as the pipe has cooled, clean, flux, and assemble the pipe and fittings for the next section and advance the trellis through the jig so that the next joints to be soldered are over the holes

5. Repeat assembling pipe and fittings, soldering, and advancing the trellis through the jig until all the duplicate rectangular sections of the trellis are done.

Assembly jig during use

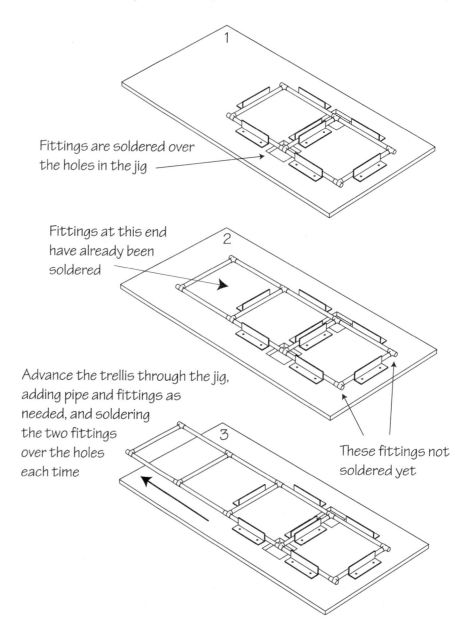

Fittings are soldered over the holes in the jig

Fittings at this end have already been soldered

Advance the trellis through the jig, adding pipe and fittings as needed, and soldering the two fittings over the holes each time

These fittings not soldered yet

Tip	Even if the plywood in your jig looks flat, it probably isn't perfectly flat. To cancel out any warp or twist in your jig, turn over the part of the trellis you have already made before assembling the next section. Do this every time you start a new section.

If your jig is warped in any direction, it will have a cumulative effect over the entire trellis and the finished trellis may lean or twist.

To compensate for any amount of warp in your jig, turn the trellis over after soldering each pair of fittings, before adding more pipe and fittings.

Clamps

Clamps may be necessary if you need to assemble pipe and fittings into a non-flat shape like an arch or an obelisk.

It is not a good idea to try to build something like an arch one piece at a time. You would not be able to tell if each piece was in correct alignment with the others.

You could try assembling all the cut pipe into all the fittings for an arch and then seeing if the complete arch was correct, but you would find that the pipes will not stay put on their own. They will twist and fall out of the fittings.

A good way to hold everything together is to use a small hose clamp around each end of each fitting. The hose clamps will provide enough of a grip between the fittings and pipe to enable you to build a complete structure, align everything correctly, and then solder the joints.

Because hose clamps exert pressure evenly all around the clamp, they won't damage the pipe or fittings like vice grips or C clamps would.

A hose clamp (or band clamp)

Get the correct size for the pipe and fittings you need to clamp (see text)

A hose clamp is also called a worm gear clamp or a worm gear band clamp. Hose clamps are available in the plumbing section of most home centers. They may be sold in "contractor packs" containing 10 clamps. It is usually a good idea to buy the contractor packs, since one trellis structure might need 20 clamps or more. Each joint of each fitting will need its own clamp. For instance, each Tee fitting will need three clamps. Hose clamps are also available at auto parts stores.

It is important to get the right size clamps so that they can exert pressure around the fittings. For ½ inch copper pipe, get clamps that are labeled with a clamping range that includes 11/16" — the approximate diameter of the fittings for ½ inch pipe. A typical clamp of this size may say "Range: 7/16-29/32". The range is usually stamped on the band of the clamp.

It is also important to use clamps that have a band that will come completely out of the adjusting screw, because you must be able to get the clamp on and off the trellis without disturbing the trellis fittings. Most clamps will come completely out of the screw. You can check for sure before purchasing clamps by loosening one clamp's adjusting screw completely and making sure the band will open up.

HOW TO USE HOSE CLAMPS

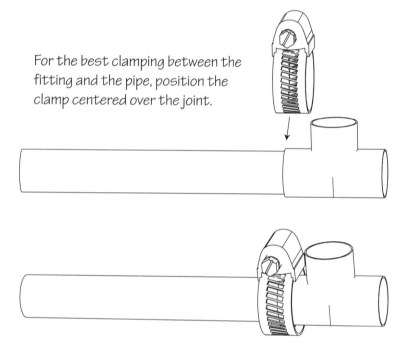

For the best clamping between the fitting and the pipe, position the clamp centered over the joint.

1. Gather all the cut pipe and fittings for your project.

2. If there is any doubt about the size or fit of any parts, do a dry fit with hose clamps before proceeding.

3. Clean and flux all pipe ends and joints.

4. Put a hose clamp over each end of each fitting, insert the pipe, and tighten the clamp around the pipe as you assemble your project. Try to put about half the width of the hose clamp band on the fitting, and half the with of the band over the pipe

5. By measuring between points on your project that should be the same distance apart, check that the final assembly with clamps is correct. Check any sections that should be a rectangle by comparing the diagonals of the rectangle as on page 30.

6. To solder, loosen all the hose clamps around **one** fitting and slide them away from the fitting. Solder all the joints. Repeat for all other fittings, one at a time.

7. Completely unscrew all the hose clamps and remove them from your project.

Tip	Use a hex head nut driver that fits the hex head screw of the hose clamp. The nut driver will be much easier to use than a straight blade screwdriver. If you have a cordless drill or screwdriver, you can use the drill with a hex head driver bit.

CHAPTER 8 *Measuring and Assembly Techniques*

In This Chapter

The dimensioning and measuring system used for the copper pipe projects in this book is explained here. Also, Rules, Tips, and Tricks for assembling copper pipe projects.

Dimensioning Explained

There are several ways dimensions could have been given in this book, including the actual length of pipe between fittings, the center-to-center distance between pipes, or the outside-to-outside distance between pipes.

This section explains the reasons for the dimensions given in this book, for those that are interested or that want to develop their own designs. If numbers make your head spin or you just want to get on with making a project, you can skip ahead to the next section.

Most projects in this book have an accompanying materials list. The materials list assumes you are making most trellises and other projects to a standard size. For simplicity, the standard size I used to develop most designs was based on multiples or parts of 12".

The 12" standard will also make it easy for you to develop your own designs that use the same dimensioning. You can easily draw designs on 1/4" grid graph paper, with each 1/4" representing 3" in the real world. When you create a design you want to build, you will be able to assemble it with the same lengths of pipe and the same measuring jigs as used in the projects in this book.

The 12" standard represents the **center-to-center** distance of the pipes. So if a pipe project is described as a 12" square, the **centers** of the pipes are 12" apart.

Because fittings take up space, you do not cut the actual pipe to the center-to-center measurement. A ½ inch diameter pipe with a fitting at each end must be cut 3/4" less than the center-to-center measurement you want. A ¾ inch diameter pipe with a fitting at each end must be cut 1" less than the center-to-center measurement.

And because ½ inch pipe is 5/8" in diameter, the **outside-to-outside** dimension of a 12" square is 12-5/8". The outside-to-outside dimension of a 12" square made from ¾ inch pipe is 12-7/8". This is usually of no concern. The only time you need to know the

35

outside-to-outside measurement is if you need to fit a trellis into a certain exact space. Usually, you want the centers of parts to align with each other. For instance, to make an arbor you might make two trellises from ¾ inch pipe with a center-to-center width of 18". An arch top you make to fit those trellises would also have a center-to-center width of 18", whether you make the arch from ½ inch pipe or ¾ inch pipe.

If you want larger or smaller trellises, or a trellis or arbor to fit into an exact space, you can modify the dimensions any way you wish. But it will be up to you to determine the dimensions to cut the pipes based on the information given above.

How To Assemble Trellises Without Measuring

The secret is to **use measuring jigs**. If you will take the time to make a measuring jig for each length of pipe used in a project, you won't need a tape measure at all when cutting pipe. And all the pipes will be more accurate because they will all be cut to the same standard. You won't have to worry about finding fractions like 11-1/4" on a tape measure, and doing that a couple dozen times while you build a project. Just do it once, to make an accurate jig, and then forget about measurements entirely.

See page 28 for information on making measuring jigs. It is easy, and well worth your time.

Of course, there are always exceptions. Some projects use lengths of pipe too long for a measuring jig, so you may need to keep your tape measure handy if you build one of those.

Now, what length to make your measuring jigs? Most of the dimensioned projects in this book list the pipe dimensions in the form "**d12**", "**d6**" and so on. "**d12**" means the center-to-center distance of the assembly you are making is 12", but you need to cut the actual pipe shorter than 12" to allow for the space taken up by fittings. ½ inch pipe fittings and ¾ inch pipe fittings take up different space, so a **d12** jig for ½ inch pipe is different than a **d12** jig for ¾ inch pipe. The table below lists the size to make each measuring jig.

If a project you want to make only uses one or two dimensions, you only need to make measuring jigs for those dimensions. Label the jigs with the pipe sizes (1/2 or 3/4) and the **d#**. Save your measuring jigs - they are permanent tools. Pretty soon you will have a whole collection and you won't need to make a measuring jig again.

Dimension Label	Jig and Pipe Length when using 1/2" diameter pipe	Jig and Pipe Length when using 3/4" diameter pipe	Center-to-Center distance between fittings
d3	2-1/4"	2	3"
d4	3-1/4"	3	4"
d6	5-1/4"	5	6"
d9	8-1/4"	8	9"
d12	11-1/4"	11	12"
d(anything)	always 3/4" less than the d#	always 1" less than the d#	the d#

Understand Tee Fittings

A Tee fitting always connects three different pieces of pipe. Pipe does **not** pass through a Tee fitting. When you see an illustration including a Tee fitting in this book, it means that you need to cut three pipes and make three soldered or glued joints.

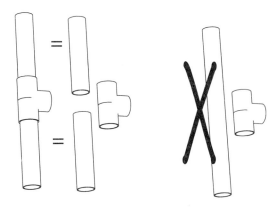

Assemble in Sections

If you are assembling a project without using a jig, always try to make sub-assemblies of parts. Make sure each sub-assembly is square and straight and the fittings are oriented in the correct direction. Solder or glue the parts for the sub-assemblies. Then attach more parts to the completed sub-assemblies.

This is especially important when using adhesives. If you try to do too much at one time without waiting for the adhesive to cure, the first parts you assemble will twist, turn, and/or come out of their fittings while you work on other parts.

Making sub-assemblies of pipes and fittings that are supposed to form squares or rectangles also helps overcome three common problems:

- The pipes are cut to slightly different sizes.
- The pipes are not fully seated in the fittings.
- The fittings accept more or less of the pipe than they are technically supposed to.

By assembling squares and rectangles, you can easily check to see if the sides are parallel and the diagonal measurements are the same. If you use an assembly jig, the jig will show you if something is wrong because either the pipes won't fit in the jig or the pipes will be loose in the jig.

Assemble Repeating Patterns

Many trellis projects are based on repeating patterns of squares or rectangles. Assemble each repeating pattern and make sure they are perfectly square and flat. Then assemble the repeating patterns to each other and make sure those assemblies are square and flat. An assembly jig as shown on page 30 does this for you automatically.

Assemble from the Inside Out

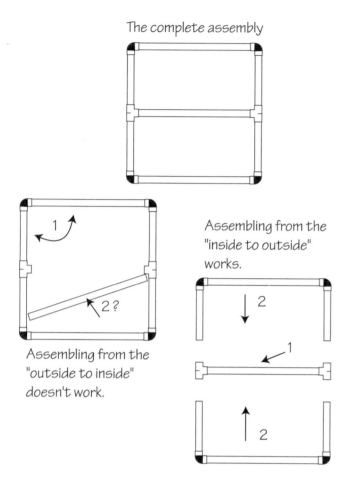

The complete assembly

Assembling from the "outside to inside" doesn't work.

Assembling from the "inside to outside" works.

A typical copper pipe project is made from pipe, Elbow fittings, and Tee fittings. The order in which you assemble these parts to each other is important. The general rule is "work from the inside to the outside".

As an example, take a look at the simple square design in the illustration. If you were to try to assemble it from the outside to inside by making the square first and then trying to put in the cross bar, you would not be able to put the cross bar between the two Tee fittings.

By putting the Tee fittings on the inner pipe first, you can then assemble the outer pipes and fittings to the inner pipe.

One of the benefits of dry fitting your projects before final assembly is that it will be obvious to you if you are trying to assemble a project in the wrong order. If you need to take any pipes or fittings apart in order to put in another pipe or fitting, it means that you are assembling in the wrong order.

Make Sure Assemblies are not Warped or Twisted

By sighting down the length of any pipe and fitting assembly, you can check if the parts are straight and flat. The illustration shows what you might see if the legs on this assembly were crooked or twisted.

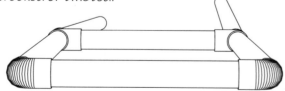

Projects assembled from pieces of pipe running between fittings can appear straight and true when actually they are warped or twisted in some manner.

You can easily check for a warp or twist by sighting down the length of anything you are assembling. If the assembly is on a table top, put your eye level at table top height at the end of the table, and sight down all sections of pipe that are supposed to be straight.

Make Sure Fittings are Facing Properly

If you assemble Elbows and Tees to pipe, and the fittings are turned even slightly in the wrong direction, you will not be able to assemble the rest of the project squarely. Every pipe that connects to the fitting that is out of alignment will also be out of alignment.

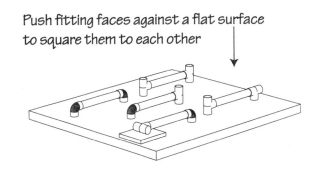

Push fitting faces against a flat surface to square them to each other

You can easily make sure Elbows and Tees are facing the same direction. After attaching fittings to the ends of a pipe, put the open face of the fittings on a flat table. You can then easily adjust each fitting so its face sits flat against the table, and the fittings will then have the same orientation with respect to each other. After you solder the fittings or the adhesive has set, every pipe connected to those fittings will be correctly oriented.

Tee fittings can be assembled at exact right angles to each other by the same technique, as shown. You can assemble an Elbow for ½ inch pipe at right angles to a Tee fitting by laying the Tee fitting on a piece of 3/8" plywood or other 3/8" shim and adjusting the face of the Elbow to sit flat on the table. Use a 3/4" inch shim for ¾ inch pipe.

Use Assembly Helpers

All projects need to have pipes and fittings held in proper alignment while you solder or while the adhesive cures. If you are not using a full size jig, you can use "assembly helpers" made from copper pipe and fittings.

An assembly helper is a temporary set of pipe and fittings used to hold parts in alignment while you solder or while adhesive sets. This assembly helper is the same size as the cross bar and will hold the long lower legs in alignment.

The illustration shows an assembly helper for a pot trellis with a cross bar. If you assemble this project without an assembly helper, you will find that the lower legs will "toe in" or "toe out", since there is nothing to hold them in position.

By using an assembly helper on the ends of the legs, the legs are held in exactly the right position. The assembly helper in this case is exactly the same as the cross bar with fittings. You do not solder or glue the assembly helper to the legs. You put it in place while you solder or while the adhesive sets on the main project, and then you remove it.

If you assemble more than a few copper pipe projects, you may find it useful to keep some standard assembly helpers that match the projects you make most often. You can solder or glue the fittings on an assembly helper to make a permanent "mini jig" if you wish.

CHAPTER 9 *How to Bend Copper Pipe*

In This Chapter

Bending Copper Pipe allows you to make a wider variety of projects than those that only use standard plumbing fittings. You can make in-line bends, compound bends, circular arcs, and elliptical arcs. By bending, you can also eliminate many fittings and the time it takes to prepare and solder the fittings.

You May Not Need this Chapter – Yet

You only need to read this chapter if you want to make projects that involve bending pipe. If you are just getting started and you haven't made any simple projects from straight pipe yet, you can safely ignore this chapter and come back to it later.

Why Bend Pipe?

Bending tools or jigs cost money and take time to make, so why go to the expense or the trouble? Here are some good reasons to bend pipe:

- Bending pipe lets you make corners without using fittings. This may make for different or more attractive designs.
- Because you can make corners without fittings, you save the cost of the fitting, plus the time and materials to cut the pieces and solder the joints.
- Bending pipe lets you make other angles besides 45 degrees and 90 degrees.
- Bending pipe lets you make long arcs, such as an arch at the top of an arbor.

Any type of copper plumbing pipe can be bent with the aid of bending tools or jigs. You **must** use a tool or jig when bending copper pipe. Bending tools and jigs support the wall of the pipe while it is being bent, resulting in a smooth bend. Without a tool or jig, the walls of the pipe are unsupported and will collapse during bending, resulting in a pipe with an unattractive kink in it.

Types of Benders

All types of copper pipe can be bent with the aid of manually operated pipe or conduit benders.

It is important to use the correct bender for the job. Some benders are only designed to bend soft copper tube. Others are designed to bend hard copper pipe. Soft copper tube is the type that comes in coils, usually in a box. Hard copper pipe is the type sold as straight 10 foot long pieces.

Also, benders are sized to fit the pipe they bend. You cannot use a bender designed to bend ½ inch pipe to bend ¾ inch pipe, and vice versa.

Most home center plumbing departments carry small pipe benders, designed to bend **soft** copper tube up to about 3/8 inch diameter. This type of bender is fine if you want to bend some decorative additions to a trellis from ¼" soft copper tube. It is useless for bending the main structural parts of a trellis, which should be made from ½ inch or ¾ inch **hard** copper pipe.

Plumbing supply companies sell pipe benders that are capable of bending larger size pipe, but once again, most of these are designed for **soft** tube. These companies will also carry or be able to order manual pipe benders capable of bending hard pipe, but these are very expensive tools.

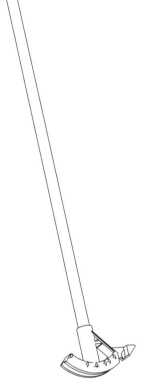

The solution in order to be able to bend the size and type of pipe you want to bend, without spending a whole lot of money, is to walk over to the **electrical** department at the home center. There you will find a device known as a **conduit bender**.

Conduit benders are made for bending the steel conduit used by electricians for running wires in exposed locations, such as on the surface of a block wall. Lucky for us, a conduit bender also works well for bending hard copper pipe.

There are different types of conduit benders. Some bend "EMT" conduit, and some are designed for "rigid" conduit.

"EMT" stands for Electrical Metallic Tubing. This type of conduit has thin steel walls, and for that reason is also called "thinwall" conduit. Rigid conduit has much heavier steel walls.

A conduit bender designed for EMT or thinwall works fine for bending hard copper pipe. You don't need to go to the expense of buying a conduit bender designed for rigid steel pipe. All conduit benders will have engraved or stamped right on the head of the bender what material the bender is designed for.

If you are bending ½ inch copper pipe, get a conduit bender that says "½ inch EMT only" or "½ inch thinwall only" on it.

If you are bending ¾ inch copper pipe, get a conduit bender that says "¾ inch EMT only" or "¾ inch thinwall only" on it.

Don't worry that the conduit bender says "only" on it. By saying "EMT only" the bender manufacturer is speaking to electricians that might use the tool, telling them that the tool is designed for EMT conduit, not the much heavier rigid steel conduit. In my experience, hard copper pipe takes about as much effort to bend as thinwall conduit, so they are probably roughly equivalent in terms of the force the bender must be able to withstand. At any rate, an "EMT" or "thinwall" bender works fine for bending hard copper pipe.

How to Use a Conduit Bender

When you buy a conduit bender, it will probably come with an instruction booklet. The instruction booklet is directed towards electricians, and covers the common types of bends they need to make. You may want to read the instructions, but don't expect to understand a lot of them unless you are an electrician. Plus, the dimensions they give are for bending EMT conduit. When you bend copper pipe the dimensions needed are slightly different. Here are the basics of understanding a conduit bender:

Tip

Some rental stores may carry conduit benders if you are not ready to buy. When you buy your first conduit bender, buy one from a manufacturer that sells complete benders with a head and handle, and also just the heads. There will be displays or boxes of these benders in the electrical department at the home center. That way you can buy a complete bender with head and handle for one size pipe, such as ½ inch pipe. Later you can just buy a head for another size pipe, such as ¾ inch pipe, and use the same handle.

Some bender handles may fit different brands of benders. If in doubt, take your bender handle to the store and try it out. The boxes of bender shoes are usually open so you can screw in your handle and see if it fits.

- First, look at your bender. On the sides there will be some markings such as "45", "60", "90", and others. These are the standard angles that electricians may need to bend. Of course you can bend any angle in between, but those in-between angles are not marked. You cannot use a conduit bender to bend angles more than 90 degrees.

The alignment pin on this particular bender is at the top. Your bender may be different.

- Next to the angle markings there will be raised lines or arrows. When you use the bender, these raised lines or arrows will line up with a pin or come to a vertical position as you bend, which tells you what angle you have bent in the pipe. Consult your bender and instruction booklet to see which method your bender uses. For example, if you want to bend a 60° angle, you bend the pipe until the raised line or arrow next to the "60" mark aligns with the pin or comes to a vertical position. Some benders have built-in bubble levels that show when you have bent to 45° or 90°.

- The shoe of the conduit bender has a curved groove and a "toe". The toe grabs and holds some of the straight pipe. The groove forms the bend.

- Near the 10° mark there will be an arrow pointing down towards the groove. This is the start mark – where you line up marks on the pipe in order to put bends in a certain place.

- The shoe of the conduit bender also has a flat or ridged foot rest or "heel" on the top back side. This is where you apply foot pressure while bending. Using your foot and your body weight at this point increases your leverage tremendously.

HOW TO MAKE A 90° BEND AT THE CENTER OF A PIPE

A 90° bend is the most common bend to make. For instance, you could make a 90° bend in order to make a corner for a trellis without needing to use two pieces of pipe and an Elbow fitting.

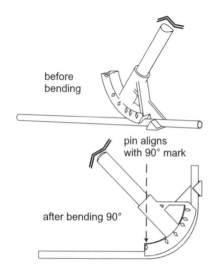

before bending

pin aligns with 90° mark

after bending 90°

Here is how to make a 90° bend, with the bend centered at a certain spot on the pipe:

1. Mark where you want the center of the bend to be. If you want the center of the bend to be in the middle of a length of pipe for instance, mark the center of the pipe.

2. Make another mark 4" away from the center mark.

3. Put the pipe on a firm level surface such as concrete. Don't bend on a wood floor (such as a deck) or you will put dents in the wood.

4. Put the pipe into the groove and through the toe on the bender, so that the bender shoe is above the center mark and the toe of the bender is towards the 4" mark you made.

5. Adjust the pipe so your **4"** mark is directly below where the start mark arrow on the bender is pointing.

6. Stand on the heel side of the bender. Pull the bender handle towards you until the bender grabs the pipe.

7. Now continue pulling the bender handle towards you slowly and evenly, and at the same time, step on the foot rest and use your body weight to apply most of the force. Your hands and arms will mostly provide control. Your foot and body weight will provide most of the bending force.

8. While you are bending, watch the line or arrow next to the 90° mark on the bender. When this mark aligns with the pin or comes to a vertical position, stop bending, and you will have a 90° bend. Do not go beyond the 90° mark, or you will start to crush or kink the pipe.

Your bend will come out **approximately** centered on your center mark. I say approximately because even slight variations in bending technique or in placing your mark at the start line will cause the bend to be off center a little bit. If you need a bend to be exactly centered, it is best to bend a longer piece of pipe than you need, and trim the ends as required to center the bend.

Notice that even though you may start a bend right at the end of a pipe, the bend will have a straight "leg" on it. This is because the bender toe must grab on to some of the pipe in order to make the bend. If you want a little less leg, you can use your tubing cutter and cut some of the leg off. If you want a longer leg, you can start your bend further back from the end of the pipe.

Also notice that the 90° corners produced by using Elbow fittings and by bending are quite different. An Elbow fitting makes a very tight corner. The 90° bend made by a bender has a larger radius. Most EMT conduit benders make a 4-1/2" radius bend in ½ inch pipe.

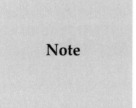

Note

All the dimensions given in this chapter for putting bends in certain spots on a pipe are only for using ½ inch copper pipe and a ½ inch conduit bender. ¾ inch pipe and a ¾ inch conduit bender will not use the same dimensions because the larger conduit bender makes a larger radius bend in the pipe.

Also, the dimensions will be a little off if you bend ½ inch EMT conduit instead of copper pipe, because ½ inch EMT has a slightly larger diameter.

HOW TO MAKE TWO 90° BENDS AT A CERTAIN CENTER-TO-CENTER DISTANCE

You might want to make two bends at a certain center-to-center distance of the **pipes** away from each other. This is different than putting the center of the **bends** in a certain place.

For example, you might want to bend a simple arch such as shown in the illustration so that the arch will fit another assembly with fittings centered 36" apart. To do this:

1. Add 6 inches to the center-to-center distance you want between the pipes. In the example, you want 36" center-to-center, so 36+6 = 42".

2. Mark a pipe **at least** 6" longer than that, or 48", with two marks, 42" apart. Put the two marks equidistant from the ends of the pipe you are using. For instance, if you are using a pipe 48" long, you would put your marks 3" from each end. The 3 extra inches on each end will give the bender toe something to grab on to and will also give your finished arch straight 3" legs, similar to the illustration.

3. Put the start mark of the bender over one of your marks on the pipe, and bend the pipe 90° toward the other mark.

4. Turn the bender around, put the start mark of the bender over the second mark on the pipe, and bend the pipe 90° towards the first bend.

5. The centers of the ends of the pipes should end up approximately 36" apart. If you don't bend exact 90° angles or you did not put the start marks on the pipe directly under the start mark on the bender, the distance may be a little off.

Tip	You normally want the two bends to be in line, without a warp or twist, so you must make sure that the first bend is standing vertically as you make the second bend. This is hard to do when working alone. If you are working on a flat level surface, you can put the first bend between two concrete blocks or similar supports so that the first bend is vertical while you make the second bend. If you make enough of these bends, it may be worth your time to devise a wooden jig to hold the first bend vertically for you while you make the second bend.

Because there are a lot of variables when bending pipe, it is very difficult to bend to an exact size. Instead of trying to bend a pipe to fit a certain exact size, it is usually better to bend the pipes first, and then fit other pipes to the pipes with bends.

For instance, if you are bending arches for an arbor, you wouldn't want to set the arbor uprights in concrete and then try to make arches to match. You would first make the arch, and then put the uprights wherever they match the arch. It won't make any difference if your arbor is actually 36-1/2" inches wide instead of exactly 36", or whatever your arch turns out to be.

How to Make Two 90° Bends as Close Together as Possible

If you want to make two 90° bends right next to each other in the center of a pipe as shown below, here is how to do it:

1. Mark the center of the pipe. Make a second mark 8" away from the center mark.

2. Put the start mark on your bender directly over the 8" mark, with the bender heel toward the center of the pipe. Make a 90° bend, which will cause a long leg of pipe to go up in the air as shown.

3. Still facing the same direction, move your conduit bender away from the first bend and put the start mark directly over the center mark. Then bend 90° again.

4. Since the pipe already had a 90° bend in it, when you make another 90° bend in the same direction, the pipe will bend around to a horizontal position as shown. The bender handle will interfere with the pipe, but you can just move the pipe so it is directly against one side of the handle.

As usual, variations in your bending technique and where you align your marks will affect the accuracy of the results. The bend may come out a little lopsided, or one leg of the bent pipe may be a little longer than the other.

Because of the radius of the conduit bender and the fact that the toe of a conduit bender must have a little bit of straight pipe to grab, the tightest arc you can bend like this will result in the finished piece having legs about 10-1/2" apart.

Also, because the bends use up some pipe, your finished piece will be about 3" less than half the length of pipe you started with. So if you start with a 72" pipe, the finished piece will be (36"-3") or about 33" tall.

The tallest arch you can make like this, starting with a full 10' pipe, is (60"-3") or about 57" tall.

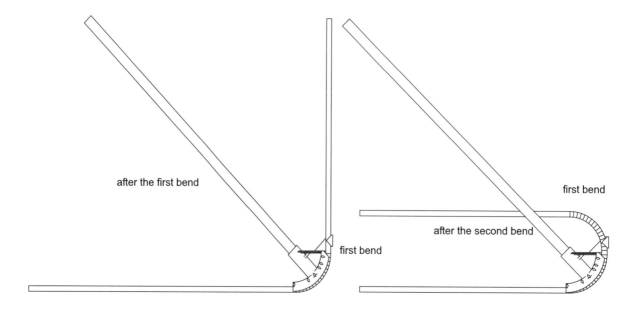

after the first bend

first bend

first bend

after the second bend

HOW TO BEND OTHER ANGLES

To bend other angles, follow the same steps as bending a 90° angle. The only difference is where you stop the bend. If you want a 60° angle, stop bending when the raised line or arrow next to "60" aligns with the pin or comes to a vertical position, depending on the system used by your brand of bender.

The illustration shows two 45° angles bent in a pipe, such as you might do to make one style of arch.

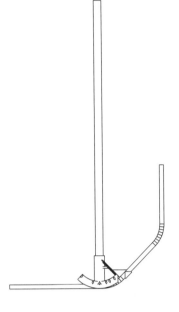

HOW TO POSITION THE BENDS FOR COMMON ANGLES

If you want to put a 45° bend centered at a certain point such as the middle of a piece of pipe, follow the instructions for putting a 90° bend at a certain point as on page 44, except make the start mark 2" away from the center mark instead of 4", and bend to 45° instead of 90° of course. The table below gives the offset distances for all the common bends when using ½ inch diameter pipe and a ½ inch conduit bender.

Angle of bend	Put your start mark this far from where you want the center of the bend
90°	4"
60°	2-5/8"
45°	2"
30°	1-1/4"
22.5°	1"
10°	1/2"

You always use your bender so that the toe of the bender is pointing away from the center of the bend.

HOW TO MAKE COMPOUND BENDS

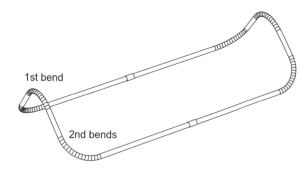

1st bend

2nd bends

A compound bend is two or more separate bends in one piece of pipe, with each bend going in a different direction. As an example, let's make the "Row Cover One" project from page 69, but this time using bends instead of fittings. By bending, we will eliminate six 90° Elbow fittings, plus 12 cuts and 12 soldered joints.

The new materials list consists of:

- (2) pieces of ½ inch pipe, 5 feet long
- (2) straight couplings

To make compound bends, it is usually best to start with the bends that are furthest from the ends of the pipe. In this case, that would be the 90° bend that is up in the air. So,

1. Make a 90° bend centered on one of the 5 foot pipes. As described previously in this chapter, to center a 90° bend you measure 4" from the center of the length of pipe and use that as your start mark. So for this project, mark the center of the pipe, which is 30" from one end, and make another mark 4" away from that. Put the start mark on your bender over the 4" mark on the pipe, with the bender heel towards the center of the pipe, and make a 90° bend.

2. Now you have an "L" shaped piece of pipe. Measure 18" from the end of each leg and make a mark for the centers of your next bends. Measure 4" away from those marks back towards the ends of the pipe, and make the start marks. (Of course you could have just measured 14" to begin with, but I am explaining it this way so you can see the procedure and apply it to your own projects.)

3. The first bend you made should be lying flat on the floor. Facing one end of the pipe, put the bender start mark directly over the start mark on the pipe. Make a 90° bend, then do the same on the other leg.

4. You should now have half of this project. Bend the other 5 foot pipe the same way, and assemble the halves with couplings. If your bends are a little off, the legs of the two bent pipes might not be equal lengths. In that case just trim off the longest leg(s) to match the others.

Tip

It can be difficult to visualize the results of a compound bend before you make the bends. To help see how a compound bend is made, you can follow through the steps in any compound bending project with a piece of soldering wire or a paperclip as a model.

Also, copper pipe is expensive enough that you probably don't want to waste it practicing bends. If you have a bending project, and want to practice the bends or find out how far apart to make some bends to get the results you want, you can use electrical conduit instead.

EMT or thinwall electrical conduit is about half the price of hard copper pipe, so you'll save some money. And, you may be able to make some utilitarian projects using the conduit after practicing your bends.

If using EMT conduit and making 90° bends, put your start marks 3-1/2" away from the center-of-the-bend mark instead of 4".

Bending Arches

DECIDING ON A BENDING METHOD TO MAKE ARCHES

Before learning to bend arches, you should know that you can bend circular and elliptical arches from either hard copper pipe or soft copper tube. Each method has its advantages and disadvantages as outlined below.

Copper Type	Tools needed	Cost of copper	difficulty	results
Hard Copper Pipe	conduit bender and (optionally) one jig for the bender	cheapest	takes more study and practice	stronger, more rigid and more dent resistant
Soft Copper Tube	a separate jig for each different arc you want to bend	much more expensive	easy	possible to bend and dent more easily

All else being equal, I suggest you bend soft copper pipe if you intend your arch or arbor to support annual plants or lightweight perennials. If you intend your arch or arbor to support heavy perennials or those that can get very heavy in time (such as some Clematis, Wisteria, Trumpet Vine, etc.), then it would be best to use hard copper pipe.

A similar recommendation goes for the size of the pipe to use. Use ½ inch pipe for lighter plants, and ¾ inch pipe for large heavy perennials.

If you intend your arch to be part of something like a row cover support, hard copper pipe is the best choice. Soft pipe may bend and dent as you move it around your yard, secure it to the ground, or store it for the winter.

If you are making utilitarian arches such as row cover supports, and you don't mind the look of galvanized steel, you can bend electrical conduit with just a conduit bender or with a jig similar to the one I will be showing for copper pipe. But you must build the jig so that it accepts conduit instead of copper pipe. EMT conduit has a slightly larger diameter than copper pipe.

If you decide to make arches by bending soft copper tube, just skip ahead to that section, on page 57.

CIRCULAR ARCH STYLES YOU CAN BEND FROM HARD COPPER PIPE

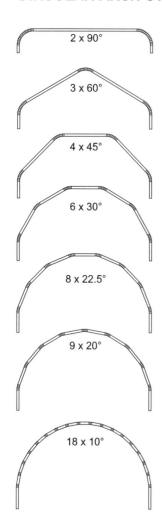

2 x 90°

3 x 60°

4 x 45°

6 x 30°

8 x 22.5°

9 x 20°

18 x 10°

The typical reason you might want to bend an arch in hard copper pipe is to make an arch for the top of an arbor. Normally, an arch is bent through an angle of 180° – at one end of the arbor the arch goes up towards the sky, and at the other end of the arbor the arch is pointing towards the ground. In other words, the arch is a semicircle.

There are many ways to bend a copper pipe through a total angle of 180°. In order to easily understand the technique for making a reasonably smooth circular bend, we can first look at some bends that don't produce a smooth curve.

First, you can make (2) 90° bends. This makes a rectangular sort of arch as shown.

You can make (3) 60° bends. This puts a steep angle in the arch.

You can make (4) 45° bends. Now you see the beginnings of a smooth arch.

Likewise, you can make (6) 30° bends, (8) 22.5° bends, (9) 20° bends, and (18) 10° bends.

As you can see, making eighteen 10° bends results in a reasonably smooth arch. After you make such an arch, you will have to look closely to tell that the arch is actually composed of eighteen straight sections of pipe.

If you want to make a smooth circular arch, you need to know the following:

• How long a piece of pipe do you need?
• Where do you put the bends in the pipe?
• How can you accurately make eighteen 10° bends?

The answers to the first two questions come from some simple math, which we will get to later. The answer to the last question is to make a simple jig for use with a conduit bender.

HOW TO MAKE AN ARCH BENDING JIG FOR YOUR CONDUIT BENDER

Using a conduit bender by itself to try to make a smooth arch, even a bender marked with 10° angles, will give poor results. A 10° angle is too small of an angle to read consistently, and you need eighteen nearly identical 10° angles to make a nice arch. So the purpose of the jig is to let you bend 10° angles accurately, and spaced evenly apart. Here is how to make the jig to use with your conduit bender:

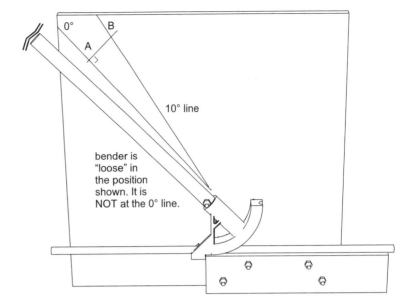

1. Get these materials:

- a piece of flat, ¾" thick plywood, 2 feet square. The home centers usually have plywood pre-cut to this size.

- Five 5/16x3" carriage bolts, with a nut and washer for each bolt, plus one extra nut.

- A 2x4. You only need 16" of the 2x4, so you may be able to scrounge a piece. Otherwise buy the shortest one you can. Sight down the lengths of the plywood and the 2x4 before buying and get the flattest, straightest pieces you can.

- The tools you need are a saw, a wrench or pliers, a drill, and a 5/16" drill bit capable of drilling steel. And you need a conduit bender. (This jig does not replace a conduit bender, it is an accessory for a conduit bender.)

2. Along one edge of the plywood, fasten a 16" piece of 2x4 as shown, with one end centered on the plywood. Use four of the carriage bolts to fasten, after drilling 5/16" holes through the 2x4 and the plywood. This part of the jig will be under a lot of pressure and screws or nails may not be sufficient.

3. In the steel handle of your conduit bender, 4-1/2" away from the bottom of the bending shoe, or as close as you can get, drill a 5/16" hole straight through the handle.

4. With the plywood on a table or flat on the floor, lay the conduit bender on the plywood. Put a piece of straight copper pipe in the bender shoe and push the bender against the 2x4, with the lip of the bender shoe around the end of the 2x4 as shown. Mark the location of the hole through the conduit bender handle. This step sets the gap to allow space for the copper pipe between the bender and the 2x4. You can make it a little easier to put pipe into the bender, and move the pipe through the bender, by adjusting your mark just a hair away from the 2x4.

5. Drill a 5/16" hole through the plywood at the mark from step 4. Put a 5/16" carriage bolt through the plywood and use a washer and nut to fasten the carriage bolt to the plywood. Now put the bender handle over the carriage bolt and use your extra nut to secure the bender handle to the carriage bolt. You may need to ream out your hole in the bender handle a bit, but you want a tight fit. This makes a pivot point for the bender.

6. Now put a piece of long straight copper pipe in the bender shoe, and pull the bender handle until the bender grabs the pipe, and if you applied any more force you would actually start to bend the pipe. The position of the bender at this point is 0°– there is no bend in the pipe, but it is just about to start bending. Make a mark on the plywood along the full length of the edge of the bender handle. It is very important to **not** mark the zero line where the bender is loose and rotated fully in the unbent direction. You must pull the bender handle so it grabs

the pipe and almost starts to bend it, then mark that as the zero line. Remove the copper pipe from the bender.

7. Now you are going to draw a line that is 10° away from the 0° or "no bend" line. You can use a protractor if you have one, but in case you don't, here is another way using measurements:

- Measure 16" from as near the pivot bolt as you can get, along the 0° line, and put mark **A**.

- Use a square, and draw a line perpendicular to the 0° line from point **A**.

- Measure 2-13/16" from point **A** along the perpendicular line and put a mark **B**.

- Move the bender handle until the edge of the handle is over point **B**. Mark along the full length of the bender handle in this position. This is the 10° line.

As you can see, what you are doing with this jig is making it easier to accurately read a 10° angle. Reading down at the bending shoe, a 10° angle is a very small movement, and very difficult to determine accurately. By transferring the angle out to the edge of the plywood, you will be able to consistently bend an accurate 10° angle.

Now you need to know how long a piece of pipe to bend, and where to put the bends.

DETERMINING THE PIPE LENGTH IN AN ARCH

For this example, assume that you want a circular arch to connect the uprights of an arbor you are building. You want the uprights to be 3 feet away from each other.

1. The length of the circumference of a complete circle is the diameter of the circle times Pi (approximately 3.14). So the length of a semicircular arch is half of that, or (half the diameter times 3.14).

2. The diameter of the semicircular arch in this example is the distance between the uprights, or 36".

3. The calculation (half the diameter times 3.14) is therefore (½ x 36" x 3.14).

4. Your calculator shows this is about 56½", so that is the length of the pipe that will be in the final arch.

5. Because a conduit bender always needs a section of straight pipe to "bend against", you need at least 12" of extra pipe. So in this case you need to start with a piece of straight pipe at least 68½" long. If you use a piece of pipe just 56½" long, you won't be able to make the last few bends. After bending your arch, use your tubing cutter to cut off any excess pipe.

You need to calculate how long the pipe in the arch is so that you can then calculate where to put the bends in the pipe. When actually bending the arch, you don't need to bend from an exact length piece of pipe. You can just bend an arch from a full 10 foot piece of pipe, and then cut off the excess.

DETERMINING WHERE TO PUT THE BENDS IN AN ARCH

For a smooth circular arch, you want to put the bends equal distances from each other.

1. To bend a half circle, you need to bend a total of 180°, so you need eighteen 10° bends at equal distances.

2. For this example, the entire length of the arch is 56½", so the distance between your bends should be (56.5 divided by 18). Your calculator shows that this is about 3.139 inches.

3. The closest any standard tape measure will be able to measure to that number is 3-1/8". Using 3-1/8" instead of the actual figure results in a ¼" total error over the 56½" length of the pipe in the arch, which is insignificant.

ARCH TABLE FOR COMMON SIZE ARCHES

I showed how to determine the length of the pipe you need and where to put the bends so that you will be able to bend any size arch you want. But to save you time in case you want to make some common size arches, I have done the calculations for you:

Arch Diameter (distance between arbor uprights)	Actual length of pipe in the arch	Minimum length of pipe needed for bending (arch length plus 12")	Put eighteen 10° bends this far apart:	Total Error
24"	37.7"	49.7"	2-1/8"**	½"
36"	56.5"	68.5"	3-1/8"	¼"
48"	75.4"	87.4"	4-3/16"	-
60"	94.2"	106.2"	5-1/4"	¼"
72"	113.1"	*	6-5/16"	½"

* A ten foot piece of pipe is long enough to make an arch with a diameter of 72", but not quite long enough to let a conduit bender make the last couple of bends. Instead, you can make nine 10° bends in two separate pipes and join them with a coupling.

** It is difficult to put bends this close together. If you want a 24" arch, you might consider making nine 20° bends, 4-1/4" inches apart.

HOW TO USE THE BENDING JIG

Using the bending jig requires a little bit of practice, and you may need to make some minor adjustments because of your individual bending style or some variations in how you built the jig.

The main thing you need to know is that hard copper pipe is somewhat springy. If you bend it to exactly the 10° line on your jig and then remove bending pressure, you will notice that the springy pipe causes the bender handle to return several degrees towards the unbent position. Here's how to get a real 10° bend:

1. With pipe in the bender, pull the bender handle so the handle goes a few degrees beyond the 10° line.
2. Release pressure and notice where the bender springs back to. It will probably be a little shy of the 10° line.
3. Carefully pull the bender handle again, using short tugging motions, and bend until the bender handle goes slightly beyond the 10° mark.
4. Release pressure and check where the bender handle springs back to. It should be just about at the 10° mark.
5. If not, repeat steps 3 and 4 until the bender handle can stay at the 10° line without the bent pipe pulling it back. You will quickly get a feel for the technique, and within a few bends

you will probably be able to make an accurate bend with just a couple pulls of the bender handle.

6. You may find it useful to fasten a stop block on your jig a few degrees beyond the 10° line. By using a stop block, you can consistently "overbend" just enough on the initial pull, without going too far. You must avoid bending too far, because a conduit bender cannot "unbend". If you do bend too far, you must remove the pipe from the bender and unbend the pipe by hand.

7. You can easily check your bending accuracy while you make your first arch. After you make nine bends, there should be a 90° (right angle) total bend in the pipe, because nine 10° bends makes 90° of total bend. If the total bend is more than 90°, you must be bending more than 10° on each bend, so adjust your 10° line back slightly towards the zero line. If the total bend is less than 90°, you must be bending less than 10° on each bend, so adjust your 10° line ahead slightly.

BENDING AN ARCH

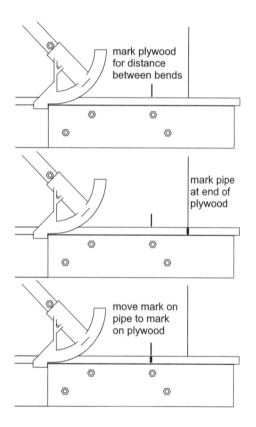

mark plywood for distance between bends

mark pipe at end of plywood

move mark on pipe to mark on plywood

Now that you know how to consistently bend an accurate 10° angle, here is how to bend an entire arch. If you follow these steps, you **do not** need to mark any measurements on the pipe ahead of time.

1. Start with a straight piece of pipe at least 12" longer than the length of pipe in the arch.

2. On the jig, make a mark on the **plywood** that represents the distance between each bend, as shown. For instance, in the example on page 52, we calculated a distance between bends of 3-1/8" to make a 36" diameter arch. Measure 3-1/8" from the edge of the plywood, and put a mark.

3. Put your pipe in the bender and align the end of the pipe flush with the end of the toe. This will make an arch with the shortest straight section possible at the end, which is about 2¼ inch on most benders. If you want longer straight sections at the ends, put the pipe in the bender so it extends beyond the toe by the amount of the straight section you want.

4. Pull the bender handle to the zero line. The pipe should be very snug in the bender at this point.

5. Before you actually bend, and with the bender handle at the zero point, make a mark on the **pipe**, directly opposite the edge of the plywood.

6. Now make your 10° bend.

7. Advance the pipe through the bender until the mark you made on the pipe lines up with the mark you made on the plywood. By doing so, you have just moved the pipe through the bender by the distance between bends. The mark on the pipe should line up with the mark on the plywood **while the pipe is snug in the bender** (the bender handle is at the zero line).

8. Repeat steps 4 - 7, seventeen more times, and you will have your arch. Do whatever you need to do to keep track of the number of bends - count out loud, make marks on paper, etc. It won't be obvious how many bends you have made just by looking at the pipe.

9. Each time you advance the pipe, just before you start bending, you must check the bent end of the pipe. The bend must always stay in the same plane, parallel to the plywood. If all your bends are not in the same plane, your arch will come out warped or twisted.

10. Depending on the size of your arch, sometime after making nine bends the bent end of the pipe may start to interfere with the bending handle. Just move the pipe to the outside of the bending handle, but keep it directly against the bending handle so all your bends stay in the same plane.

11. If you started the pipe flush with the bender toe, you will have a short straight section of pipe about 2¼" long at the beginning of the arch. You can add the same length of straight section to the other end of the arch before you trim the excess. If you started with a longer section of straight pipe, add that longer length to the other end before trimming.

While you make your first arch, you will probably feel like you could use a few more hands. Here are a few things you can do if needed:

- Get a helper to hold the pipe in the right plane and hold the jig steady.

- Attach some "outriggers" to the jig so it is more stable and you don't need to hold it in order to keep it upright.

- Attach the jig in an upright position to a piece of plywood laying flat on the ground, with angle brackets. Then you can stand on the plywood while bending and keep everything steady.

- If you have a large table or workbench, you can clamp or bolt the jig to the top of the table and work in a horizontal position. Support long pipes with sawhorses or the rungs of a stepladder.

ELLIPTICAL ARCH STYLES YOU CAN BEND FROM HARD COPPER PIPE

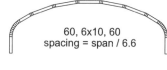

60, 6x10, 60
spacing = span / 6.6

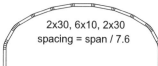

2x30, 6x10, 2x30
spacing = span / 7.6

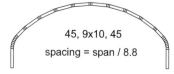

45, 9x10, 45
spacing = span / 8.8

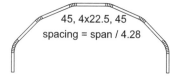

45, 4x22.5, 45
spacing = span / 4.28

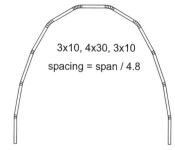

3x10, 4x30, 3x10
spacing = span / 4.8

Similar to the way you can bend a circular arch from equally spaced 10° bends, you can bend elliptical shapes, but by bending different angles at equal spacing.

A few examples are given in the illustration. The numbers are the bends in the pipe. For instance, 60, 6x10, 60 means that the first bend is a 60° bend, followed by six 10° bends, and ending with another 60° bend.

All the arches shown have a straight length of vertical pipe at each end.

The spacing between bends is shown in the illustration. As an example, say you want your ellipse to span about 36". If you make the first style of ellipse shown, the spacing is the span divided by 6.6.

36" divided by 6.6 is about 5.452, so you would put your bends about 5-1/2" apart.

Then, to get an even ellipse, you should bend from each side towards the center. For example, for the first elliptical style shown, you would bend 60, 10,10,10 from one end, and 60,10,10,10 from the other end. Any minor discrepancy will then come out in the top center of the ellipse where it won't be noticeable.

The bends in a smaller size span may be too close together to allow bending a single pipe from both ends, because a conduit bender needs some straight pipe to bend against. If the spacing is less than 10", you can bend two separate pipes with the bends that make up half an arch, and then cut and connect the two pipes with couplings at the top center.

As for circular arches, it is best to bend the elliptical arches you need first and then make other parts fit the actual size of the arch, rather than trying to bend an exact-size arch.

How to bend arcs from soft copper tube

Soft copper tube can be bent by hand, without the use of a bender, but you still need to make and use some sort of a jig, for two reasons:

- To make the exact curve you want.
- To bend the tube evenly and without kinking.

HOW TO MAKE PLYWOOD BENDING JIGS FOR SOFT COPPER TUBE

A plywood bending jig will be a permanent tool. Make a plywood jig if you need to bend the same curve more than once, or you just want the greatest accuracy. Skip ahead to "Other ways to bend soft copper tube" if you only need a couple of arches and/or don't care if they aren't exact.

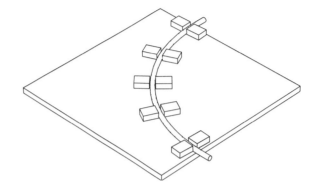

You need to make a separate jig for each different curve you want to make. A jig for a 36" diameter arc will not form a 48" diameter arc, and a jig for a circle will not form an ellipse. But, you can use the same piece of plywood for the base of more than one jig, and make the parts that do the shaping removable and replaceable by fastening them to the plywood with bolts or screws.

Here are the steps in making a jig:

1. Determine the size of the plywood you need. To make a circular arch, all your jig needs to do is allow you to form about half of the arch. Then you can advance the tube and form the rest of the arch. To make an elliptical arch, your jig needs to allow you to form half of an elliptical arch. Then you can turn the tube over and form the second half. I have already figured the size of a piece of plywood you need to make a jig using those techniques, to the nearest foot:

Arch type and size	Size of plywood base needed for jig
Circular 36"	2 foot square
Circular 48"	3 foot square
Circular 60"	3 foot square
Circular 72"	4 foot square
Elliptical 36"	2 foot square
Elliptical 48"	2 foot by 3 foot
Elliptical 60"	2 foot by 3 foot
Elliptical 72"	3 foot by 4 foot

2. If you are making a jig for a circular arch, draw one half of the arch, which will be one quarter of a circle. Use one corner of the plywood base as the center of the circle. If you are making a jig for an elliptical arch, draw one half of that arch. See the last page of this chapter for how to draw an ellipse.

3. The line represents the **center** of the pipe in the arch. Use a small piece of pipe centered over the line as a gauge, and fasten small blocks of wood such as pieces of 1x2, about 4 inches apart with the ends of the blocks directly against the side of the gauge pipe.

4. Directly opposite each block of wood, attach another block of wood against the other side of the gauge pipe.

This method of making a jig makes it easy for people without special tools. If you have a jigsaw or bandsaw, you can form the curves of the arch with curves cut from plywood instead of using blocks of wood.

USING THE BENDING JIG

Soft copper tube comes in coils that have tighter curves than the arch you are forming. So really you are going to be "unbending" the coiled tube and forming it with your jig.

1. Take the coiled tube out of the package, and starting with the outside end of the tube, carefully "feed" the tube into your jig by pressing the tube between the first two forming blocks, then uncoiling a little more tube and pressing it between the next two forming blocks, and so on. Keep the curve in the tube in the same plane it had in the package - don't let it jump out of the jig and start curving up in the air.

2. When your jig has formed as much of the shape as possible (which should be a half of a circular or elliptical arch), remove the tube from the jig.

3. To complete a circular arch, put the end of the curve you already made in the first set of blocks, and form the rest of the arch just like the first part.

4. To complete an elliptical arch, turn over the half arch you have already made, put the midpoint of the arch over the midpoint of the jig, and form the second half of the arch by working the tube into the jig towards the second endpoint.

5. Uncoil a little extra tube, and check your work. A circular arch should conform to the jig any way you lay it. Both halves of an elliptical arch should conform to the jig, but you will only be able to check one half at a time and then turn it over to check the other half.

6. At the end of the arch, mark the point to cut the tube. Double check this point before cutting the tube. If you are making a 36" diameter arch for instance, the center of the pipe at the cut point should be 36" away from the center of the other end of the tube. Small variations of ¼ inch or ½ inch are normal, but if the measurement is off by more than that you should try to adjust the arch by re-forming it in the jig.

7. For ultimate precision, you can draw an accurate full size arch on a concrete floor or on paper templates, then compare your formed arch to the ideal, and make whatever adjustments are necessary.

OTHER WAYS TO BEND SOFT COPPER TUBE

If you only need one or two copies of the same arch, it may not be worth the trouble or expense to make a permanent plywood jig. You can use the following methods to make temporary "jigs". Helpers will be valuable if you use these techniques.

1. If you have some flat lawn, you can lay out the full size arch using wooden stakes or pieces of rebar pounded in the ground vertically. Then carefully form the copper tube against the stakes. Get a helper to keep the tube from shifting while you form it. To make the layouts:

• For a circular arch, run string the length of the radius from a stake at the center point, and pound in other stakes every 6 inches or so around the arch.

• For an elliptical arch, lay out the ellipse in the same way, but by using string that goes around the focal points of the ellipse (see the last page of this chapter).

2. If you have a large concrete floor, you can draw the full size arch by using the washable chalk made for kids to draw on sidewalks. Then, with several helpers, form the tube to match the arch. Or you can put some heavy weights like concrete blocks on the tube at intervals as you form it.

3. If you have odds and ends of scrap lumber, you can make a full size temporary jig. Draw the full size arch on a flat concrete floor (or use full size paper templates indoors). Arrange the lumber with the ends of the pieces around the arch, similar to the way the bending jig was made. The lumber should all have the same basic dimension, such as all 1x2s or all 2x4s. Then lay a couple of longer pieces across all the lumber and fasten with screws. Form the copper tube against this large jig. You can use weights or helpers as needed to keep the jig and the tube in place.

4. You can form circular arches with stakes and a single piece of wood that represents the radius of the arch. Measure the radial distance from the end of a piece of 1x2 or 2x4 and drill a hole for a pivot point. On a flat lawn, pound a piece of rebar through the pivot point. Form tube against the end of the wood, and pound stakes on either side to keep it in place. Rotate the wood around the pivot a little more, and repeat. To use this method indoors, you can make a pivot with a bolt through a piece of plywood. As you form the arch, put heavy weights on the tube to keep it in place.

MAKING FREE FORM ARCHES OR OTHER SHAPES FROM SOFT COPPER TUBE

Soft copper tube can be hand formed any way you like. For instance, you could set up the uprights for an arbor, start some tube at one side, and free form any sort of curve in the tube while you uncoil it towards the other upright.

This kind of total free forming can lead to some unexpected (either good or bad) results. You need to be especially careful not to put any sort of kink or sharp bend in soft copper tube. Once the tube has kinked, it will not be possible to smooth it out again.

Since soft copper tube is too expensive for most people to experiment with, a better technique would be to draw your designs first and see if you like how they look. All designs for soft copper tube should have smooth flowing curves, no sharp angles or tight bends.

Once you get a design you want to make, you can transfer it to full size templates and form the tube to the template.

Using your arches in an arbor

Arches for even the smallest arbor should have cross bars connecting the two arches for bracing and support. Without cross bars connecting the arches, an arbor can easily lean and twist, especially if it will be covered by a large plant that creates wind resistance, or if the arbor gets bumped or moved. So now that you have gone to all the trouble of making nice arches, the best way to use them is to cut them up and add fittings!

Here is the reason to make complete arches, and then cut them: for a typical arbor that uses two arches, you will get a perfect complete arch if you make two complete, identical arches, then cut them at the identical locations, add Tee fittings, and add cross bars to connect the arches.

The other alternative would be to try to separately form each bent pipe in both arches. It is very difficult to make six or eight separate but identical bent pipes, so your finished arch would probably be warped or twisted in some way.

Here is how to add cross bars between two arches:

1. Make two identical arches. Lay one on top of the other **and** also stand them side by side to compare them, and make any necessary adjustments to them so that they are as close to identical as possible. If the arches are identical in curve, but one is taller than the other, you can mark and cut the legs of the taller one to match the shorter one. If you cannot make your arches identical with minor adjustments, consider making another arch to match the best one. Your completed arch will only be as good as the parts used to make it. Arches with different curves or different heights will cause the cross bars in the completed arch to appear tilted and twisted. And if the arches have different widths, you will either have trouble attaching the completed arch to your uprights, or the uprights will appear to "toe in".

2. If you are making a circular arch, you can determine how many cross bars you need and the distance between them from the table below. The table makes the assumption that your arbor uprights have a cross bar close to the top of the upright, so your arch does not need another cross bar right at the ends. If you are making an elliptical arch, you can use the table to get the approximate distance between cross bars and then adjust to get even spacing if you wish.

Diameter of arch (distance between arbor uprights)	Length of pipe in the arch	Option 1 - all spacing approximately 18-7/8"	Option 2
24"	37.7"	1 bar	2 bars, spacing ~ 12-5/8"
36"	56.5"	2 bars	4 bars, spacing ~11-5/16"
48"	75.4"	3 bars	5 bars, spacing ~12-5/8"
60"	94.2"	4 bars	7 bars, spacing ~11-3/4"
72"	113.1"	5 bars	8 bars, spacing ~12-5/8"

Option 1 uses wider spacing and fewer bars, option 2 makes a stronger, more rigid assembly and uses as many bars as necessary to achieve an approximate 12 inch spacing. You may wish to use approximately the same spacing that you are using in the uprights of the arbor, normally 12 or 18 inches.

3. To mark the spacing between bars on the arch, you can cut a piece of string to the length of the spacing, and then use the string to lay out the positions of the bars on one arch. If you made your arch from 10° bends with a conduit bender, there will be eighteen short straight sections of pipe. Try to adjust the spacing so you will cut through a straight piece of pipe - it will help the Tee fittings seat more easily.

4. With the two identical arches standing up next to each other and in perfect alignment, wrap some tape around them at several points to hold them in position, but don't cover your layout marks.

5. At your layout marks, scribe lines square across both arches. Remove the tape from the arches and cut the arches at the scribed lines.

6. Insert a Tee fitting and a cross bar at each bar position. The length of the cross bars is determined by the width of the uprights in your arbor, and would normally be the same length as the cross bars in your uprights.

7. You can do a dry fit of the arch in its upright position by using hose clamps as shown on page 33. For accuracy, work on a flat level surface.

8. When everything looks right, finish the arch assembly by soldering or using adhesive.

9. Attach the arch assembly to your uprights, also working on a flat and level surface, and checking that the arbor is plumb and square before doing the final assembly between the arch and uprights.

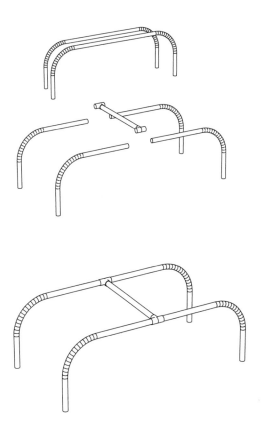

How to draw an ellipse

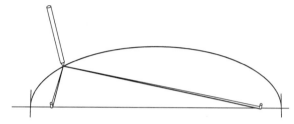

To draw a full-size ellipse, get a piece of cardboard, poster board, foam board, or plywood a little larger than the full size ellipse will be.

1. Draw a straight line with endpoints that represent the width of the arch you want. If you want a 36" wide arch, draw a straight line and mark the endpoints 36" apart.

2. Put pins or nails at the endpoints. Get some string, loop it around the pins, and tie a knot so the loop runs straight from pin to pin, with only a bit of slack.

3. Move the pins equal distances from the endpoints towards the center of the line. For instance, move each pin 2" towards the center. These are the "focal points" of the ellipse.

4. Put a pencil to the side of both pieces of string (not inside the loop), and trace out an ellipse from one endpoint of the line to the other, keeping the string taut.

5. If you like the shape, you're done. If not, move the pins to other positions and draw other ellipses. Moving the pins closer to the center makes the ellipse more circular. Moving the pins further from center makes the ellipse flatter.

CHAPTER 10

First Projects

The projects in this chapter are a great way to practice your cutting and assembling skills for copper pipe, and make some useful garden structures at the same time.

How to Use this Chapter

In this chapter I will demonstrate several simple projects, and along the way, introduce you to the format used for describing projects so you can easily get all the information you need.

This chapter assumes you already know how to cut pipe (See page 9). Before building a project, decide if you want to use soldering or adhesives to assemble the project. Read the chapters about soldering or using adhesives, and then make one of these simple projects to practice those techniques.

Every project will have one or more illustrations so you can see what you will be building.

Most projects will have a materials list, like this:

- a number of pieces of pipe, cut to this size.
- this number of these type of fittings.

Most projects will have assembly notes, like this:

1. do this first.
2. do this next.

It may be worth reading the assembly notes for all these projects even if you don't actually build the project. To avoid repetition, I will explain any special techniques fully in the first project that uses the technique, and from then on assume that you know how to use that technique.

Terms Used in Assembly Notes

To avoid long explanations in assembly notes, here are the terms I will be using and what they mean:

Hard copper pipe. Hard copper pipe is the type sold as straight 10 foot long lengths of pipe. The dimension given, such as "½ inch" hard copper pipe, refers to ½ inch pipe diameter. For making projects larger and stronger, you can use ¾ inch hard copper pipe, but some dimensions may be different.

Soft copper tube. Soft copper tube is the type sold as coiled tubing, usually in a box. The diameter dimension is as for hard copper pipe.

Pipe. If the materials list just says you need pipe, you can assume it means "the same type of pipe already mentioned", which will usually be "½ inch hard copper pipe".

Fittings. Fittings for copper pipe are named and explained on page 7.

Cut. To cut means to use your cutting tool (typically a tubing cutter) and cut the pipe to the length given. See page 10 for how to use a tubing cutter. "2 pipes cut to 12"" means you will need to cut two pieces of pipe 12" long from a longer pipe in your stockpile.

Ream and clean. To ream means to remove any metal burs from the outside ends of copper pipe.(If you use a tubing cutter, there will not usually be any outside burs that would interfere with a fitting.) For trellis building, you don't need to do anything about burs on the inside of copper pipe. To clean means to use a cleaning tool or sand cloth to remove the oxidation from the outside ends of copper pipe and the inside ends of fittings. See page 13 for complete information about reaming and cleaning.

Dry Fit. To dry fit means to put together all the cut pipe and fittings for a project, but without any flux, solder, or adhesive. The purpose of dry fitting is to make sure everything fits together properly before doing the final assembly. Sometimes the illustration for the project will show an "exploded" view in order to show how the project is assembled. As you get to the more advanced projects, there may not be an exploded view because it will be obvious to you by that time how pipe and fittings go together.

Clamp. To clamp means to use any of the techniques given in **"Measuring Jigs, Assembly Jigs, and Clamping"** on page 27 in order to hold your project together while you are working on it. You must normally clamp or use an assembly jig for a project while you do a dry fit; otherwise the pipes may rotate or fall out of the fittings. If you are soldering, you can clean and flux everything, clamp all the joints in the final position, and then solder all the joints one by one. If you are using adhesives, you can put adhesive on each joint and clamp the joints one by one as all the parts are assembled.

Assemble. To assemble means to permanently assemble the parts of the project, using solder or adhesive.

Plant Poles

Here is an extremely simple but useful project, and good for practicing your soldering too. A plant pole is a straight length of pipe with end caps on each end.

The length of the plant pole is up to you. You could put a two foot long plant pole in a pot to support a small ivy above lower growing plants. You could make a five foot plant pole to support peas or beans in your garden. You could combine several plant poles into a teepee type trellis.

This project demonstrates the first use of an end cap.

Materials list:

- One piece ½ inch hard copper pipe, length of your choosing. Remember that 8 or 12 inches of this length may be underground or buried in a pot when you use the pole.
- 2 end caps

Assembly Notes:

1. Cut the pipe to size.
2. Ream and clean the outside of the pipe at both ends and clean the inside of the end caps.
3. Dry fit the end caps on the ends of the pipe. In this case, the dry fit is to make sure that the pipes don't have any burs that would interfere with assembly. Also, if the end caps or the ends of the pipe got dented during storage or cutting, the end caps might not fit.
4. Do the final assembly with solder or adhesive. If you solder, your plant pole is ready for use as soon as the soldered joints cool. If you use adhesive, set the pole where it won't be disturbed during the curing time of the adhesive.

Support your finished plant pole with any of the techniques given in **"How to Support Copper Pipe Garden Ornaments"** on page 147.

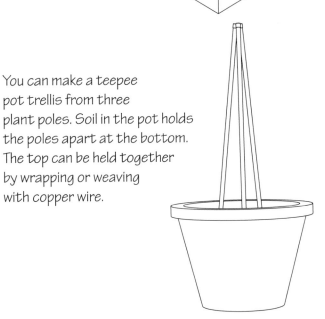

The plant pole is a single length of pipe with end caps on each end. The illustration shows a portable plant support made from a plant pole and a concrete block, with concrete to hold to pole in place.

You can make a teepee pot trellis from three plant poles. Soil in the pot holds the poles apart at the bottom. The top can be held together by wrapping or weaving with copper wire.

Plant Poles for Pots

The feet are straight lengths of pipe attached to the bottom of the plant pole with a Tee fitting.

total length of feet must fit in your pot

On these projects, the bottom of the plant pole will get some "feet". The feet provide better support when you use the pole in a pot. For instance, you can embed the feet in concrete, or put weights such as broken concrete or brick on the feet in order to stabilize the pole.

This project demonstrates the first use of a Tee fitting.

Materials list:

- One piece ½ inch hard copper pipe to make the main pole, length of your choosing. Remember that 8 or 12 inches of this length may be below soil level when you use the pole.

- Two pieces of pipe about 3" long. Before cutting these pieces, take a look at the illustration for this project and make sure that the "feet" will fit in the pot you intend to use. You can use longer or shorter feet as you require.

- 1 Tee fitting, 3 end caps

Assembly Notes:

1. Cut all pipes to size.
2. Ream and clean all pipe ends and clean the inside of all fittings.
3. Dry fit all parts.
4. Do the final assembly.

Read the information in **"How to Support Copper Pipe Garden Ornaments"** on page 147 about how to use and support your plant pole. From now on, you can assume that any project you make will need some form of support, and I may not specifically mention it again.

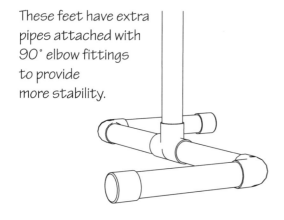

These feet have extra pipes attached with 90° elbow fittings to provide more stability.

With this variation, the bottom of the plant pole will get different "feet". Use this design if you don't want to embed a pole in concrete. The feet go at right angles to each other, and will provide the pole with good support and resistance to tipping just by burying the feet at the bottom of the pot.

This project demonstrates the first use of a 90° Elbow fitting.

Materials list:

- One piece ½ inch hard copper pipe to make main pole, length of your choosing.

- Four pieces of pipe about 3" long. Before cutting these pieces, take a look at the illustration for this project and make sure that the "feet" will fit in the pot you intend to use. You can use longer or shorter feet as you require.

- 2 90° Elbow fittings, 1 Tee fitting, and 3 end caps

Simple Pot Trellis

This is about the simplest design that could be called a trellis. It consists of two vertical pieces and one cross bar at the top. The two vertical pieces are intended to go underground by six or eight inches at least.

I won't give specific dimensions for the verticals or the cross bar because they can be varied to suit a wide range of conditions. You can make a short narrow trellis for a pot, or a tall wide trellis for the yard or garden.

If you intend the trellis to fit in a specific pot, make the cross bar at least a couple inches shorter than the smallest inside diameter of the pot, and plan on using some feet on the bottom of the legs as shown previously.

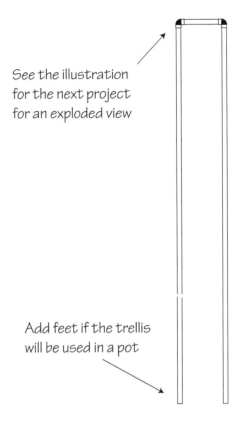

See the illustration for the next project for an exploded view

Add feet if the trellis will be used in a pot

Materials list:

- Two pieces of ½ inch hard copper pipe to make the verticals, length of your choosing, but the same length.
- 1 pipe to make the cross bar at the top
- 2 90° Elbow fittings

Assembly Notes:

1. Cut all pipes to size.
2. Ream and clean all pipe ends and clean the inside of all fittings.
3. Dry fit all parts. Refer to the illustration to see how everything goes together.
4. Do the final assembly.

Variations of the Simple Pot Trellis

Instead of plain vertical pipes, you can use any of the "feet" designs given previously. Add feet to the trellis if you plan on using it in a pot. The feet will greatly increase the stability of the trellis.

Simple Pot Trellis with a Cross Bar about 6"W x 48"H

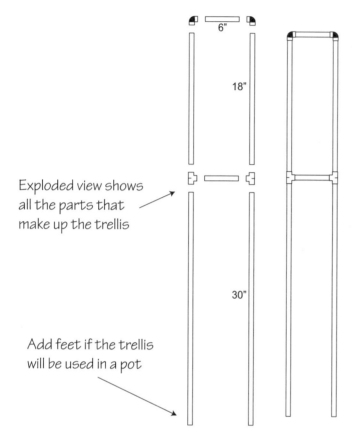

6"

18"

30"

Exploded view shows all the parts that make up the trellis

Add feet if the trellis will be used in a pot

This project will modify the design of the basic trellis by adding another cross bar. To people unfamiliar with how copper pipe is assembled in fittings, the finished project looks like it just has another piece of pipe. But as you can see from the exploded view, the project actually involves three more pieces of pipe, two more fittings, and six more joints to solder.

This time I will give specific dimensions for making a small pot trellis, but you can make the same design with any dimensions you wish. To make the design narrower or wider, you would change the length of the cross bars. To make the design taller or shorter, you would change the combined size of the vertical pieces. And to put the cross bar at a different height, you would change the lengths of the vertical pieces.

Remember if you intend the trellis to fit in a specific pot, make the cross bar at least a couple inches shorter than the smallest inside diameter of the pot.

Materials list:

- 2 pieces of ½ inch hard copper pipe 30" long to make the bottom verticals
- 2 pipes 18" long to make the top verticals
- 2 pipes 6" long to make the cross bars
- 2 90° Elbow fittings, 2 Tee fittings, 2 end caps (or add feet as shown previously)

Assembly Notes:

1. Cut all pipes to size, ream and clean as usual.
2. Dry fit all parts. Refer to the illustration and the exploded view to see how everything goes together. If you haven't already done so, this is a good time to read page 39, which shows how to hold the parts of a trellis like this in alignment while you build it.
3. Do the final assembly.

As always, you can make feet for the bottom of the verticals instead of using end caps. Or you can leave the feet open to accept rebar supports. To avoid any more repetition, I may not mention this again. Whatever design of trellis you make, think of how you will be supporting it (See **"How to Support Copper Pipe Garden Ornaments"** on page 147) and modify the design as needed.

Row Cover Support One about 36"W x 9"H x 17"D

This project makes a long narrow row cover support. You can use the finished project to support garden fabrics or plastic sheet that provide a little extra freeze protection, or wind protection, or protect young seedlings from being washed out by heavy rain. You can also use the project to support shade cloth and give new transplants an environment with less intense sunlight.

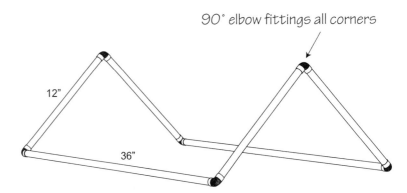

Note	This project introduces the idea of a "one piece project". The whole project is made from a single 10 foot length of pipe cut to the sizes shown in the materials list. That means — just one piece of pipe to pick up at the store, and nothing leftover when you are done.

Materials list:

This is a "one piece project" — start with a single 10 foot length of pipe.

- Cut four pieces of pipe 12" long.
- Cut the remaining pipe exactly in half. The two pieces will be about 36" long, but not necessarily exactly that long. That is why you should cut the remaining pipe in half — if you cut to a measurement you might wind up with one pipe 36" and one pipe 35¾".
- 6 90° Elbow fittings.

Assembly Notes:

1. Cut all pipes to size, ream and clean as usual.
2. Dry fit all parts. Refer to the illustration to see how everything goes together.
3. Do the final assembly. The best way to assemble is to first assemble the two large "U" shapes on a flat table. Then assemble the "U" shapes to each other with Elbow fittings.

You can use special clamps or fasteners sold in gardener's catalogs to secure your row cover material to the finished support. I don't worry about the looks too much and just use extra large "binder clamps" available from any office supply store. Take a scrap piece of pipe with you when you go to buy the clamps so you can get the size that fits the pipe.

Row Cover Support Two about 24"W x 4"H x 21"D

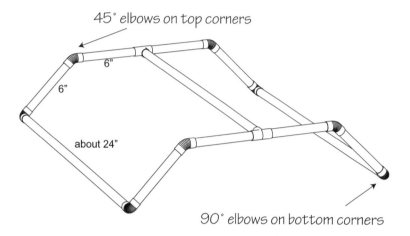

45° elbows on top corners

6"

6"

about 24"

90° elbows on bottom corners

This project makes a shorter, wider, much lower row cover support than the previous project. It also includes a top bar to better support your row cover material.

This is the first project that uses 45° Elbow fittings.

Materials list:

This is a "one piece project" — start with a single 10 foot length of pipe.

- 8 pipes cut 6" long
- Cut the remaining pipe exactly in thirds. Refer to the previous project for the reason why "in thirds" instead of an exact measurement.
- 4 90° Elbow fittings
- 4 45° Elbow fittings
- 2 Tee fittings

Assembly Notes:

1. Cut all pipes to size, ream and clean as usual.

2. Dry fit all parts. Refer to the illustration to see how everything goes together.

3. Assemble the pieces for the top, that make an "I" shape, on a flat surface. Don't use the 45° Elbows yet.

4. Assemble the pieces for the two "U" shaped sides on a flat surface, still without the 45° Elbows.

5. Now assemble the two sides to the top with the 45° Elbows.

Tip	As shown in this project, you should always assemble all the flat sections you can first, then assemble the flat sections to each other. This lets you do as much assembly as possible on a flat level surface, which should eliminate the problem of pipes being "warped" in relation to each other.

Row Cover Support Three about 48"W x 12"H x 28"D

This project makes a larger row cover support.

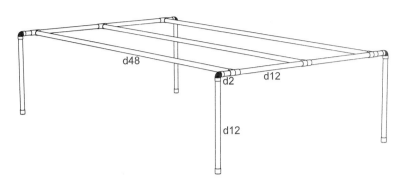

d48

d2   d12

d12

d12

Materials list:

- 8 pipes cut to **d12**
- 3 pipes cut to **d48**
- 4 pipes cut to **d2**
- 4 90° Elbow fittings
- 6 Tee fittings
- 4 end caps

Assembly Notes:

1. Cut all pipes to size, ream and clean as usual.
2. Dry fit all parts. Refer to the illustration for a good assembly method.

The easy way to assemble projects like row cover support three

First make the flat rectangular section. Before soldering, make sure it is square by checking the diagonal measurements.

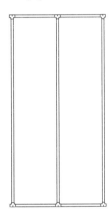

Then make four leg assemblies and attach to the rectangle.

About the d# Dimensions

This is the first use of the **d#** standard for giving pipe dimensions. As a reminder, I will use **d#** dimensions in this book so that you can make projects from either ½ inch diameter pipe or ¾ inch diameter pipe.

The pipe itself is always cut 3/4" less than the **d#** for ½ inch pipe, and 1" less than the **d#** for ¾ inch pipe.

The reason for the **d#** is that often pipes and fittings must total a certain center-to-center length. Since ½ inch pipe fittings take up less space than ¾ inch pipe fittings, giving a specific pipe length in inches wouldn't work for both sizes of pipe.

There is a more complete explanation of dimensioning on page 35.

Tip	Consider **not** soldering the leg assemblies to the rectangular frame. That will provide for easier storage of the row cover support during the off season. Or you can use the project as a row cover support early in the season, and the rectangular part of it as a trellis later in the season. For use as a row cover, hold the legs to the rectangular part with hose clamps, as shown on page 34.

Post trellis about 6"W x 54"H

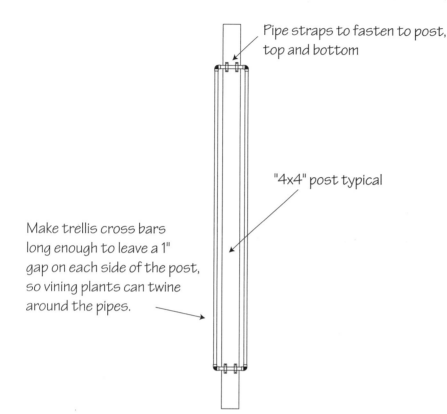

Pipe straps to fasten to post, top and bottom

"4x4" post typical

Make trellis cross bars long enough to leave a 1" gap on each side of the post, so vining plants can twine around the pipes.

This project is a good way to turn a post into a trellis. Some vines can climb a post, but most vines would prefer to have a smaller diameter support. By putting a simple trellis like this on one or two sides of a post, you can encourage most vines to find their way up the post.

The dimensions given for this project are for mounting the trellis to a typical "4x4" wooden post, which actually measures 3½" x 3½".

This project shows the first use of copper pipe straps.

Materials list:

You can make this any size you like, but as given here, this is a "one piece project" — start with a single 10 foot length of pipe.

- Cut two pieces of pipe 6" long.
- Cut the remaining pipe exactly in half.
- 4 90° Elbow fittings
- 4 copper pipe straps to fasten the trellis to the post

Assembly Notes:

Refer to the illustration and assemble the parts as usual, on a flat surface.

About Brass Screws

Use brass screws to fasten the copper pipe straps to the post. Throughout this book, I will mention using brass screws with copper pipe, because they are the most corrosion resistant when in contact with copper.

If you use steel or galvanized screws in contact with copper, there will be a reaction between the two metals which will cause the steel or galvanized screws to corrode quickly.

Brass screws are a bit of a specialty item in most home centers, so you may need to ask where they are kept. Brass screws are also available through woodworker's supply catalogs.

Pot Trivets

This project makes a very simple trivet for a large pot. The trivet lifts the pot and allows space for the pot to drain. Because the fittings are slightly bigger than the pipes, the trivet will also allow a little bit of air circulation under the pot. Air circulation and stability will be better if you make the trivet big enough so the trivet corners extend an inch or so beyond the bottom of the pot.

Materials list:

- 4 pipes cut to the same length. The length can be whatever fits a pot you need a trivet for.
- 4 90° Elbow fittings

Assemble as usual on a flat surface.

The second trivet shown lets you lift a pot up a little bit, like a miniature plant stand. You can cut the pipes to whatever lengths fit a pot you want to support, and however high off the ground you want to support it, within reason.

Materials list:

- 8 pipes cut to the same length to make the top. To get the length you can arrange four Tee fittings and four Elbow fittings in the pattern shown. Spread them apart until you get a size that will support the bottom of one of your pots. Then measure the length of pipe you need between the Elbows and the Tees. Add 3/4" to the measurement to account for the pipe that goes into the fittings.
- 4 pipes to make the legs, cut to the same length. 1" pipes for the legs are about the minimum.
- 4 90° Elbow fittings
- 4 Tee fittings
- 4 end caps

Assembly Notes:

1. If soldering, clean and flux all the parts and assemble the whole trivet, making sure it sits level. Then solder all the joints.
2. If using adhesive, apply adhesive to each joint as you assemble. Start by assembling all the pipes to the Tee fittings. Then assemble two Elbows to one Tee fitting and two Elbows to another Tee fitting. Finally, assemble the open ends of the Elbows to the other Tee fittings. Make sure the trivet sits level and allow the adhesive to cure.

CHAPTER 11 *Trellis Designs*

In This Chapter

Trellises can be used to support any type of vine or climbing plant in pots, against a fence or wall, along a deck, in your vegetable garden, or free standing in your yard. Two rectangular trellises can also be used as the uprights to begin making an arbor.

Before You Begin

All the trellis designs shown in this chapter can be modified to suit your particular needs. Before making any trellis, think about how the trellis will be used and how you will support it. See **"How to Support Copper Pipe Garden Ornaments"** on page 147 for details about supporting your trellis projects.

- If the trellis will be in the ground or supported on a deck, you may not need a cross bar along the bottom edge.

- If the trellis will be fastened to an overhead beam, you may need to modify the top of the trellis in order to reach the beam, as shown on page 153.

- If the trellis will be supported with rebar in the legs, you don't want to use end caps on the legs.

- If the trellis will be supported by burying the legs underground, you will need to make the legs 12-18" longer.

- If the trellis will be mounted against a fence or wall, you may need to incorporate some "stand offs".

- If the trellis will be in a pot, you may want to add some "feet" for support as shown on page page 66.

- If the trellis is actually going to serve as the uprights for an arbor, you may not need a cross bar at the top, or you may need to use Tee fittings instead of Elbows.

Simple or Fancy?

This chapter shows lots of trellis designs. Some of them are simple squares in different arrangements. Others are fancier and include rectangles, bending, and other shapes.

75

Here are some things to consider before deciding on a simple or fancy design:

- Simple designs are easier to make. Most of the parts can be cut to a standard size, and the trellis can be accurately assembled with the aid of a jig as shown in **"Measuring Jigs, Assembly Jigs, and Clamping"** on page 27.

- Since many trellises will be covered with vines and leaves during the growing season, there may be no reason to make a fancy design if it is going to be hidden anyway.

- If the trellis will be used in your vegetable garden, you may just want the easiest to make utilitarian type of trellis.

- If the trellis will be used near your deck or patio or in front of your house, you may want a design that looks attractive all by itself during the off season.

- If you need to fill a large space such as alongside a deck, you can make many simple designs look fancier by placing individual trellis panels next to each other and either offsetting the design up or down, or turning panels end for end or top to bottom. Some examples of this are included in the illustrations. You can also photocopy the designs in this book and play around with different arrangements on paper before you actually build anything.

Assembly Notes

Most trellises are shown as rectangles, but you can add an arched top if you wish. The techniques for making arches are shown in the chapter on bending copper pipe. An arched top can usually be added just by using Tee fittings at the top corners instead of Elbows, and attaching the arch to the Tee fittings.

Remember to always "dry fit" your projects before final assembly. Maybe a dimension isn't correct, or maybe you cut a pipe a little short or a little long. The time to find out is **before** you start soldering everything together.

Many trellis designs are based on a repeating pattern. It is always a good idea to cut enough pipe for one part of the repeating pattern and dry fit that part before cutting all the rest of the pipe. If a dimension or measurement is wrong, you will have only a few miss cut pipes instead of dozens.

This chapter assumes you have already made some of the "first projects" as shown in the previous chapter, and know how to assemble pipe and fittings by soldering or using adhesive. If you don't, please read those chapters now and practice making some smaller projects. In this chapter, I will only comment about assembly techniques if there is something unusual about a particular project.

Dimensioning - What the d# Means

All the projects shown can be built from ½ inch diameter pipe for a lightweight trellis, or ¾ inch diameter pipe for a heavier, stronger trellis. ½ inch fittings and ¾ inch fittings take up different space, so if I gave dimensions in inches each project would need two sets of dimensions. Instead of cluttering the drawings with dimensions in inches, all dimensions are given in the form "**d#**". ½ inch pipe is cut 3/4" shorter than the **d#**. ¾ inch pipe is cut 1" shorter than the **d#**.

Instead of remembering these allowances in inches and using a tape measure, make your trellis building easier and more accurate by using measuring jigs that match the pipe diameter you will be using. Please see **"Measuring and Assembly Techniques"** on page 35 for a more information.

Plant Pole with Wire

This project shows how you can make a plant pole with built-in plant ties. You can also bend and shape the wire in any way you wish for a decorative effect as well as a plant support.

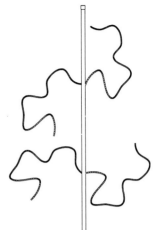

Materials List

- 1 piece ½ inch hard copper pipe cut to 48" or a length you prefer
- 6 gauge bare copper electrical wire
- 1 end cap
- If needed, pipe and fittings to make feet as shown in the previous chapter

To fasten the wire to the pole, drill 11/64" holes (for 6 gauge wire) through the pole, then insert the wires. Fasten by wrapping the wire several turns around the pole or by solder or adhesive.

If you don't want to drill holes, you can clean and flux the pipe and wire where they will join, wrap the wire tightly around the pipe, and solder the wire to the pipe.

Pot Trellis Ladder

This project is intended to support light weight vines. The small diameter cross bars are not copper pipe, but heavy electrical wire. Assemble the wire to the uprights as on the previous project.

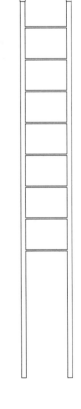

Materials List

- 2 pieces ½ inch hard copper pipe cut to 48" or a length you prefer
- 1 piece pipe cut for the cross bar at the top, make sure the length will allow the trellis to fit into whatever pot you will be using.
- 2 90° Elbow fittings
- 6 gauge bare copper electrical wire

Pot Trellis by Bending

This project makes a wide pot trellis - at least 10-1/2" wide because that is about the narrowest you can make in ½ inch pipe with most conduit benders. You will need a fairly large pot to accept a trellis with that diameter. Or you can use the trellis in the ground, and make the bends further apart if you want a wider trellis.

Materials List

- 1 piece ½ inch hard copper pipe, start with a full length if you can

Mark the center of the pipe, then mark 8" away from the center. Starting at the 8" mark, make a 90° bend. Make another 90° bend starting at the center mark. The technique for making bends close together like this is illustrated on page 46.

After you have the bends, you can cut the pipe off at equal lengths to make the trellis whatever height you prefer. Remember to allow extra length to be buried in a pot or underground for support.

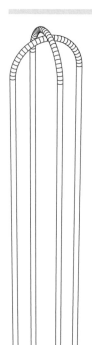

Pot Trellis Four Way

See the previous project, and use two pieces of pipe instead of one. You can attach these trellises together at the top by wrapping with copper wire with or without soldering, or drill a hole from the underside and fasten with a brass screw. The legs of this design should be long enough to reach the bottom of a pot or go underground.

Add feet for extra support in a pot. See page 66 for more information about making feet.

Pot Trellis Connected Top

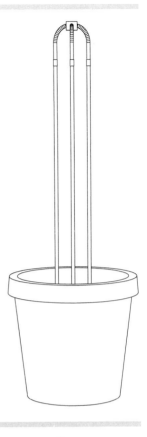

This trellis features three legs with bends at the top, joined with a circular block of wood or plastic lumber, or a ready made wood or plastic finial you can find at the home centers.

Materials List

- 3 pieces ½ inch hard copper pipe cut to 48" or a length you prefer
- 3 pieces pipe with a right angle bent in each
- 3 straight couplings

To assemble, cut the pipes with the right angle bends to any point on the bend. Use most of the bend to make a wider trellis, or only a part of the bend to make a narrow trellis as shown. Assemble the bent pipe to the straight pipe with couplings. Assemble the other ends of the bent pipes into 5/8" holes drilled in a finial of your choosing. Fasten with construction adhesive, or screws into the pipe from the underside of the finial, or both.

You can also bend the top pipes by hand by using soft copper tube.

Teepee Trellis about 3'W x 5'H

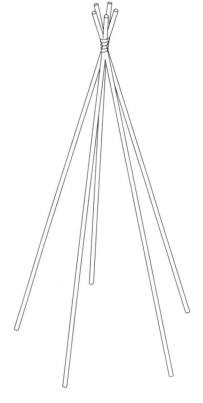

Materials List

- 5 pieces ½ inch hard copper pipe cut to 60" or a length you prefer.
- 6 gauge bare copper wire
- 5 end caps
- Assemble end caps to the copper pipes. Bundle the pipes on the ground and wrap rope or string around the end of all the pipes that have the end caps. Stand the bundle up, spread out the legs, and wrap and/or weave the top of the poles tightly with copper wire. Remove the rope or string.

Bury the legs about 6" in the ground for extra sturdy support.

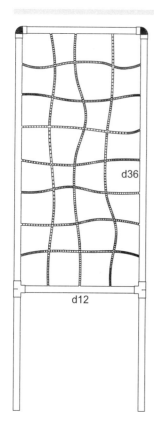

Trellis Frame about 12"W x 48"H

This frame is simple to make, and when you add wire or plastic mesh to the opening, it will provide plenty of support for lightweight annual vines. This is the first project in this chapter that uses a standard dimension (**d#**) as explained in **"Measuring and Assembly Techniques"** on page 35.

Materials List

• 4 pipes cut to **d12**

• 2 pipes cut to **d36**. As a reminder, when using ½ inch pipe you always cut the pipe 3/4" less than the **d#**, so this pipe would be cut 35-1/4". When using ¾ inch pipe, you always cut the pipe 1" less than the **d#**, so if you use ¾ inch pipe for this project, the pipe would be cut to 35".

• 2 90° Elbow fittings and 2 Tee fittings

Assemble the copper pipe frame as shown. For the mesh, you can use copper wire as shown on previous projects. Copper wire can be woven and/or soldered where the wires cross. Or use plastic coated fencing or all-plastic fencing, available at any home center. The mesh materials can be fastened to the frame by using electrical wire ties, available in the electrical department of the home centers. As you make trellises and arbors, remember that you can use this technique anytime a plant needs more support than just the copper frame of the trellis or arbor you make.

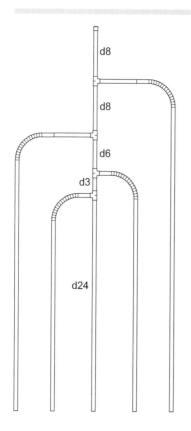

Flat Waterfall about 18"W x 49"H

Materials List

• 1 pipe cut to **d24**

• 2 pipes cut to **d8**

• 1 pipe cut to **d6**

• 1 pipe cut to **d3**

• 4 pipes with 90° bends

• 4 Tee fittings

• 1 end cap

Make the central pole first, with the Tee fittings facing in the directions shown. Then, instead of trying to bend pipes with exact measurements, just make four pipes with 90° bends and arrange them next to the fittings on the central pole in a way that you like. Then mark where to make the cuts, cut the pipes and assemble the bent pipes into the Tee fittings. Last, cut the legs to the same length, leaving extra for underground support if needed.

Basic Squares each square 12" x 12"

Materials List

- For each square, 3 pipes cut to **d12**.
- Plus 1 pipe for a bottom cross bar if you will be using one, also cut to **d12**.
- 2 90° Elbow fittings for each top or bottom cross bar.
- Tee fittings as needed for the height you make.

This is a very basic design for a trellis, but very functional. This is an excellent design if you want to make lots of trellises with different heights. Use the assembly jig described on page 30 to make this design quickly and accurately.

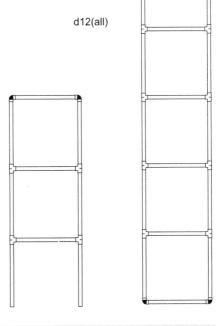

d12(all)

Basic Squares Offset

Materials List

- pipe cut to **d12**, as many as needed for the height you make.
- pipe cut to **d6** to make the half bars as shown.
- 90° Elbow fittings as needed
- Tee fittings as needed

This is a variation of the previous project showing how you can improve the visual interest of even a basic trellis by offsetting the design.

You can increase the width of this design by as many "squares" as you like, if you want to fill a large area such as alongside a deck. Or make as many "Basic Squares" trellises as you like, and support them next to each other.

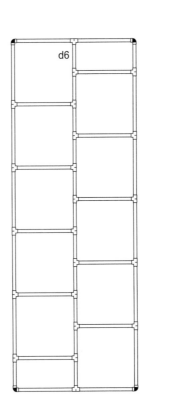

d6

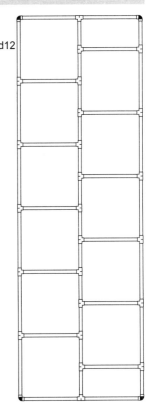

d12

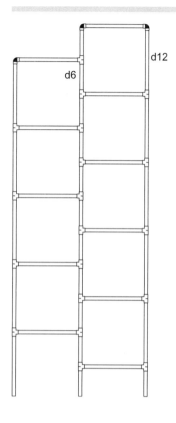

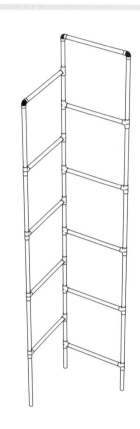

Basic Squares Angled

Materials List

- 21 pipes cut to **d12**
- 12 pipes cut to **d6**
- 90° Elbow fittings as needed
- Tee fittings as needed

This project demonstrates how you can use Tee fittings to angle one part of a trellis away from another part. This type of trellis makes a good support for tomato plants, if the trellis itself is well supported. A "T" post at the corner will provide good support.

You can even make the Tee fittings act like a long hinge by **not** soldering the top and bottom of the Tee fittings that come to the center pole from one side of the trellis.

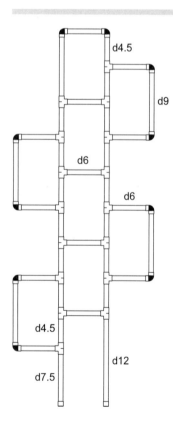

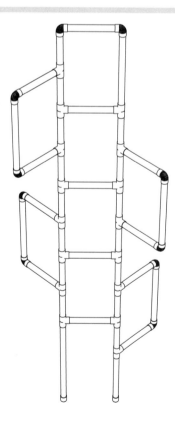

Saguaro Pot Trellis
about 18"W x 48"H

Materials List

- 1 pipe cut to **d12**
- 5 pipes cut to **d9**
- 1 pipe cut to **d7.5**
- 13 pipes cut to **d6**
- 15 pipes cut to **d4.5**
- 10 90° Elbow fittings
- 16 Tee fittings

You can make this trellis flat or turn some of the "branches" as shown before final soldering.

Basic Squares Fan

about 5'W x 5'H

Materials List

- 18 pipes cut to **d12**
- 8 pipes cut to **d8.5(-)**
- 20 pipes cut to **d6**
- 16 pipes cut to **d3**
- 4 90° Elbow fittings
- 28 Tee fittings
- 16 45° Elbow fittings

Assemble all the squares as shown. Then fit the angled parts to the squares and do a complete dry fit before permanently assembling any angled parts. The pipes marked **d8.5(-)** should be cut a hair short of **d8.5**. Cut one and do a dry fit on one section, then cut the others to match it.

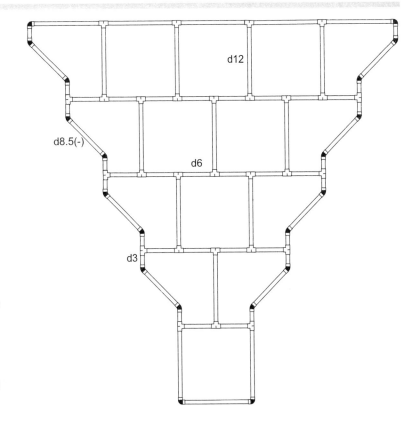

Fancy Squares about 24"W x 78"H

Materials List

- 6 pipes cut to **d18**
- 8 pipes cut to **d12**
- 45 pipes cut to **d6**
- 20 90° Elbow fittings
- 26 Tee fittings

Remember to use the inside-to-outside assembly rule. Assemble all the inner squares first. Then assemble the "spokes" from the inner squares, but without the outer Tee fittings. Then assemble the inner squares to each other. And last, assemble the outside pieces and Tee fittings to the spokes, starting at one end and working towards the other.

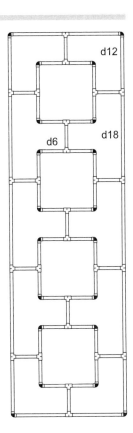

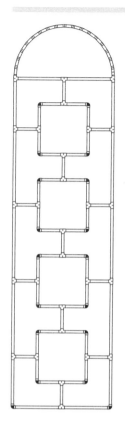

Fancy Squares Arched Top

See the previous project for materials and assembly technique. You can make the arched top by bending hard copper pipe or soft copper tube, as explained in the Bending chapter. A circular arch is shown, but you can make any style arch with a span of 24". The chapter on Arches and Arbors shows additional arch styles.

Remember that you can add an arched top to most any trellis design. In this case, the two 90° Elbows at the top corners are replaced with Tee fittings and the arch is assembled to the Tee fittings.

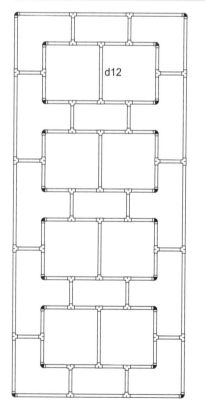

Fancy Squares Doubled about 36"W x 78"H

This project will really test your assembly skills. For that reason, you may not want to attempt it as a first project.

Working from the inside out, assemble Tee fittings to the center vertical bars. Then assemble the rectangles around the center vertical bars. Then add the spokes that radiate out from the rectangles, but without Tee fittings on the ends facing outwards. Then assemble the rectangles to each other. Last, assemble the outer pipes and Tee fittings, working from one end of the trellis to the other.

See the "Fancy Squares" project for most of the **d** locations.

Materials List

- 6 pieces pipe cut to **d18**

- 14 pieces ½ inch hard copper pipe cut to **d12**

- 66 pieces pipe cut to **d6**

- 20 90° Elbow fittings and 44 Tee fittings

Narrow Diamonds about 24"W x 99"H (or make half for 24"W x 48"H)

Materials List

- 2 pipes cut to **d24**
- 8 pipes cut to **d18**
- 6 pipes cut to **d12**
- 8 pipes cut to **d8.5(-)**
- 32 pipes cut to **d6**
- 5 pipes cut to **d3**
- 8 90° Elbow fittings, 8 45° Elbow fittings, 30 Tee fittings

Assemble the cross bars that are inside the diamonds. Then assemble the diamonds around the cross bars. The **d8.5(-)** dimension means the angled parts of the diamond should be cut a hair short of **d8.5**. Dry fit half of a diamond to check the size, then cut the other angled parts the same. After you have two diamonds, assemble the spokes from the diamonds, and then assemble the outer parts of the trellis, working from one end to the other.

As shown, this trellis is over 8' tall. If you use **d15** pipes instead of the **d18** pipes, you can reduce the height by a foot, to 87". For a 48" tall trellis, just make one of the large rectangles.

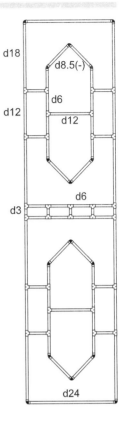

Wide Diamonds about 51"W x 99"H

This is the same trellis design as shown above, using the same parts, but doubled in width. It makes a very tall and wide trellis, and should have good support at the top and bottom such as between a deck and pergola, against a wall, or in a sturdy frame.

Only the different dimensions are labeled - some of the **d18** pipes become **d6** and **d12** pipes, plus some extra **d3** pipes and Tee fittings connect the two halves.

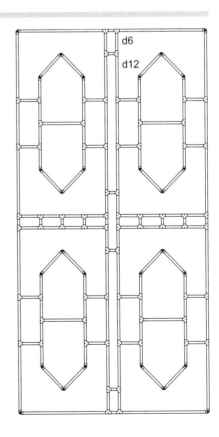

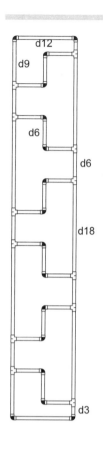

Zig Zag Plain Panel about 12"W x 72"H

Materials List

- 5 pipes cut to **d18**
- 2 pipes cut to **d12**
- 2 pipes cut to **d9**
- 23 pipes cut to **d6**
- 2 pipes cut to **d3**
- 16 90° Elbow fittings
- 12 Tee fittings

Assemble all the inner "zig" and "zag" shapes, then work from one end of the trellis to the other and assemble the outer parts to the zigs and zags.

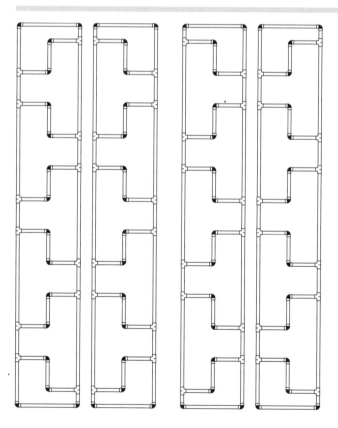

Zig Zag Plain Panels Combinations

A demonstration showing effects you can achieve by reversing trellis panels and placing them next to each other. You do not have to connect the panels, but you could if you wanted to, as shown on the "Wide Diamonds" project.

Materials for each panel are the same as the previous project.

Zig Zag Panel Variation about 12"W x 72"H

Materials List

- 7 pipes cut to **d12**
- 12 pipes cut to **d9**
- 18 pipes cut to **d6**
- 12 pipes cut to **d3**
- 16 90° Elbow fittings
- 22 Tee fittings

A stronger variation of the Zig Zag Panel because the **d18** pipes have been replaced with **d3** and **d9** pipes and extra **d12** cross bars added in between.

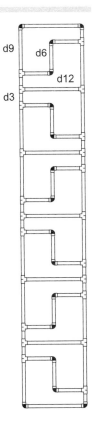

Zig Zag Variation Combination

The illustration shows the effect of four Zig Zag Variation panels arranged next to each other.

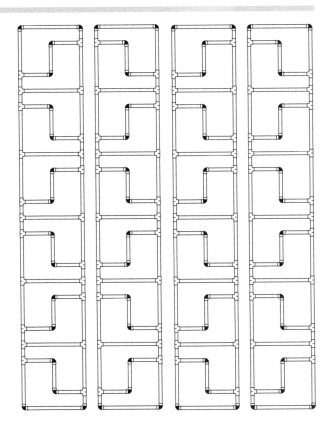

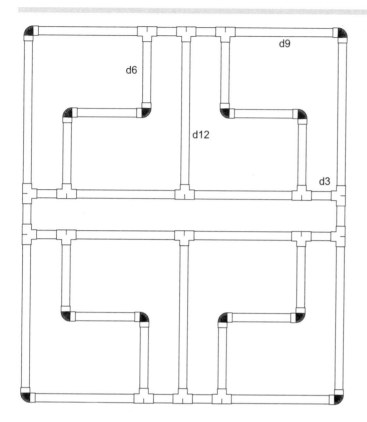

Zig Zag Medallion

about 24"W x 27"H

Materials List

- 6 pipes cut to **d12**
- 8 pipes cut to **d9**
- 12 pipes cut to **d6**
- 10 pipes cut to **d3**
- 12 90° Elbow fittings
- 16 Tee fittings

This is a decorative design you could use on a fence or wall. You could arrange several of these along a diagonal or any other pattern to support long twining vines such as Clematis.

You could also add legs and use it as a standard trellis.

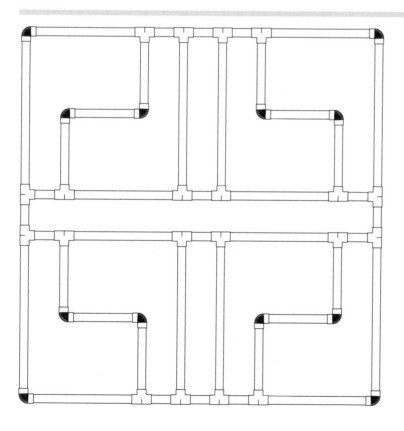

Zig Zag Medallion Variation

about 27"W x 27"H

A variation of the above project using extra **d12** and **d3** pipes and Tee fittings.

Zig Zag Fancy Medallion

about 27"W x 27"H

Materials List

- 4 pipes cut to **d12**
- 8 pipes cut to **d9**
- 20 pipes cut to **d6**
- 16 pipes cut to **d3**
- 12 90° Elbow fittings
- 24 Tee fittings

Another stronger variation of the medallion due to extra pipes and fittings.

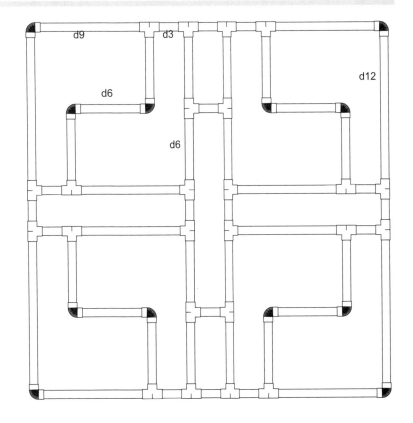

Zig Zag Fancy Turned and Stacked

about 27"W x 87"H

Materials List

- 4 pipes cut to **d12**
- 24 pipes cut to **d9**
- 72 pipes cut to **d6**
- 56 pipes cut to **d3**
- 28 90° Elbow fittings
- 88 Tee fittings

This trellis has the medallions from the previous project turned 90° and stacked three high.

The pipe locations are as shown on the previous project, with some of the **d12** pipes replaced by two **d6** pipes, and **d3** pipes connecting the medallions.

As shown, this trellis is over 7' tall. You can make a 57" tall version by stacking two "Zig Zag Fancy Medallions" instead of three.

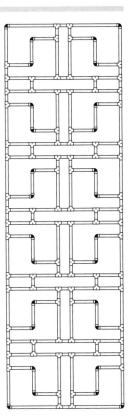

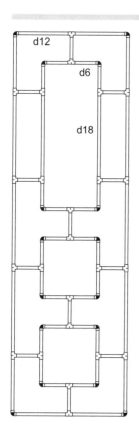

Rectangle Over Squares about 24"W x 78"H

Materials List

- 8 pipes cut to **d18**
- 8 pipes cut to **d12**
- 36 pipes cut to **d6**
- 16 90° Elbow fittings
- 24 Tee fittings

Assemble the squares and the rectangle, assemble them to each other, add the spokes from the squares and rectangles but without the outer Tee fittings, and then assemble the outer parts of the trellis, working from one end to the other.

If you want "Squares over Rectangle", just turn over the completed trellis.

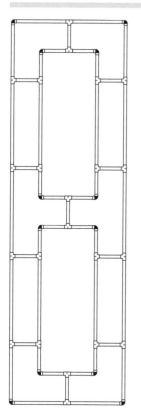

Two Rectangles about 24"W x 78"H

Materials List

- 10 pipes cut to **d18**
- 8 pipes cut to **d12**
- 26 pipes cut to **d6**
- 12 90° Elbow fittings
- 22 Tee fittings

Pipe dimension and assembly technique are as shown on the previous project.

Tall Rectangle about 24"W x 78"H

Materials List

- 12 pipes cut to **d18**
- 8 pipes cut to **d12**
- 18 pipes cut to **d6**
- 8 90° Elbow fittings
- 20 Tee fittings

Another variation on the rectangle theme. Pipe dimensions and assembly technique is similar to the previous two projects.

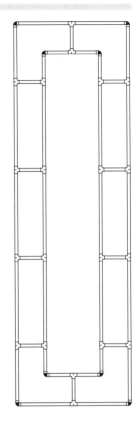

Short Rectangle about 24"W x 60"H

Materials List

- 8 pipes cut to **d18**
- 8 pipes cut to **d12**
- 16 pieces pipe cut to **d6**
- 8 90° Elbow fittings
- 16 Tee fittings

See previous projects for pipe dimensions and assembly technique.

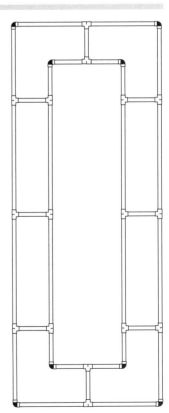

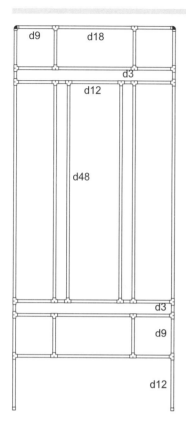

Mission Style about 36"W x 84"H

Materials List

- 6 pipes cut to **d48**
- 4 pipes cut to **d18**
- 4 pipes cut to **d12**
- 20 pipes cut to **d9**
- 8 pipes cut to **d3**
- 2 90° Elbow fittings
- 26 Tee fittings

If made from ½ inch diameter pipe, this design is rather flimsy and needs good support at top and bottom. If the trellis will be free standing it would be better to use ¾ inch diameter pipe.

You can reduce the height and increase the strength of this project by replacing the **d48** pipes with a smaller size.

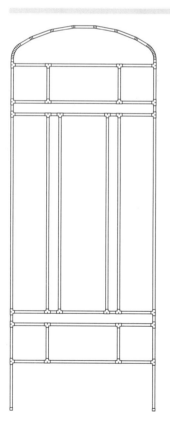

Mission Style Arched Top 36"W x 93"H

This is the same as the previous project, but with an arched top.

The arched top as shown is made with a 60° bend at each end, and six 10° bends in between. It has a span of 36". More information about making this type of arch is given on page 56.

See **"How to Bend Copper Pipe"** on page 41 for more information on bending pipe, and see **"Arches and Arbors"** on page 109 for other arch designs.

Vertical Rectangles about 24"W x 60"H

Materials List

- 5 pipes cut to **d24**
- 14 pipes cut to **d12**
- 16 pipes cut to **d6**
- 4 pipes cut to **d3**
- 2 90° Elbow fittings
- 24 Tee fittings

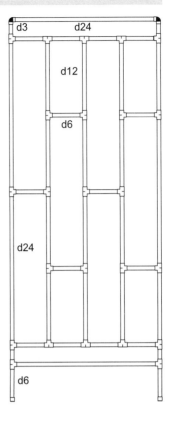

Vertical Rectangles with Narrow Top

about 18"W x 66"H

Materials List

- 4 pipes cut to **d24**
- 8 pipes cut to **d12**
- 2 pipes cut to **d9**
- 19 pipes cut to **d6**
- 10 pipes cut to **d3**
- 6 90° Elbow fittings
- 24 Tee fittings

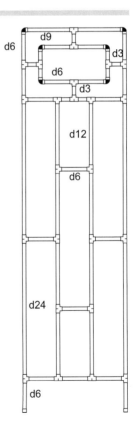

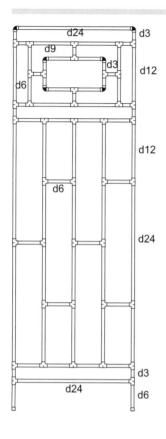

Vertical Rectangles with Wide Top

about 24"W x 75"H

Materials List

- 5 pipes cut to **d24**
- 16 pipes cut to **d12**
- 4 pipes cut to **d9**
- 24 pipes cut to **d6**
- 18 pipes cut to **d3**
- 6 90° Elbow fittings
- 40 Tee fittings

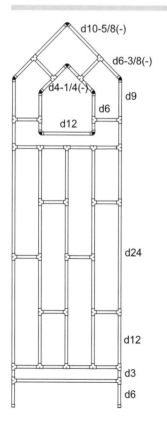

Vertical Rectangles Pointed Top

about 24"W x 84"H

Materials List

- 4 pipes cut to **d24**
- 15 pipes cut to **d12**
- 2 pipes cut to **d10-5/8(-)**
- 2 pipes cut to **d9**
- 4 pipes cut to **d6-3/8(-)**
- 22 pipes cut to **d6**
- 4 pipes cut to **d4-1/4(-)**
- 4 pipes cut to **d3**
- 4 90° Elbow fittings, 4 45° Elbow fittings, 32 Tee fittings

The rectangular part of this project is straightforward. The pointed top is difficult because the dimensions for the angled parts don't work out to be "tape measure" sizes. The nearest tape measure size is given (remember to subtract the standard amount to allow for fittings), but you should cut the pipes a little short and dry fit all the parts that involve the 45° fittings.

Expanding Rectangles

about 18"W x 54"H per trellis, two shown

Materials List

- 4 pipes cut to **d18**
- 4 pipes cut to **d12**
- 32 pipes cut to **d6**
- 4 90° Elbow fittings
- 26 Tee fittings

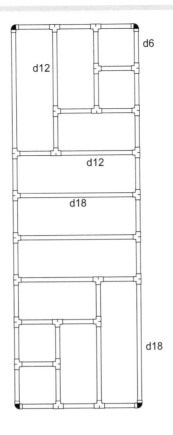

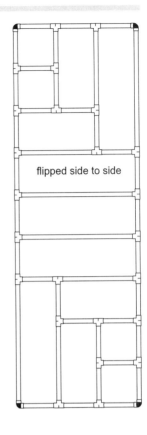

flipped side to side

Expanding Rectangles Variation about 18"W x 54"H per trellis

Materials List

- 2 pipes cut to **d18**
- 4 pipes cut to **d12**
- 40 pipes cut to **d6**
- 4 90° Elbow fittings
- 28 Tee fittings

This version of the previous project is a little stronger because of the additional **d6** pipes and fittings replacing some of the longer pipes.

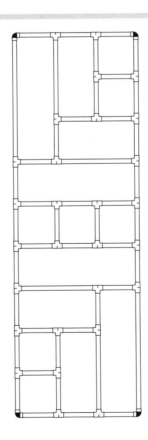

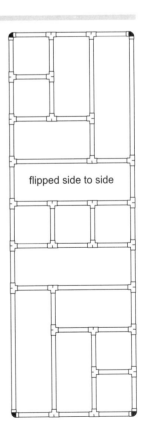

flipped side to side

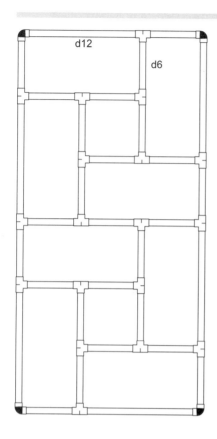

Rosette about 18"W x 36"H

Materials List

- 6 pipes cut to **d12**
- 25 pipes cut to **d6**
- 4 90° Elbow fittings
- 18 Tee fittings
- Assemble the small inner squares first, then the spokes but without Tee fittings on the outside, then the center bar that connects the two halves, then work from the center towards the ends adding the outside parts.

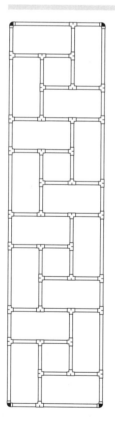

Rosette Stacked about 18"W x 72"H

Materials List

- 10 pipes cut to **d12**
- 51 pipes cut to **d6**
- 4 90° Elbow fittings
- 38 Tee fittings

Two of the previous project stacked and connected.

Diagonals about 12"W x 48"H

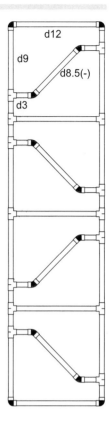

Materials List

- 5 pipes cut to **d12**
- 8 pipes cut to **d9**
- 4 pipes cut to **d8.5(-)**
- 16 pipes cut to **d3**
- 4 90° Elbow fittings
- 8 45° Elbow fittings
- 14 Tee fittings
- Cut a **d8.5(-)** pipe a little short of **d8.5**. Dry fit a complete square section with a diagonal and make sure you can make it square, then cut the other diagonal pipes to match the first pipe. Assemble the diagonals, then start at one end and work towards the other assembling all the other parts

Diagonals Two Panels

To show the effect of two "Diagonals" trellises placed next to each other.

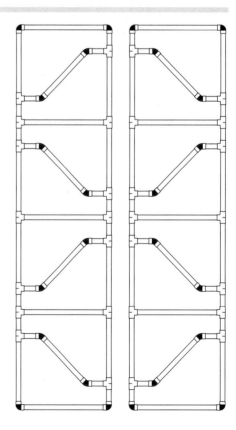

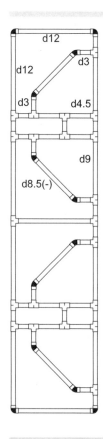

Octagon Panel about 12"W x 54"H

Materials List

- 7 pipes cut to **d12**
- 4 pipes cut to **d9**
- 4 pipes cut to **d8.5(-)**
- 8 pipes cut to **d4.5**
- 22 pipes cut to **d3**
- 4 90° Elbow fittings
- 8 45° Elbow fittings
- 22 Tee fittings
- This is very similar to the "Diagonals" Project on the previous page. See that project for assembly tips.

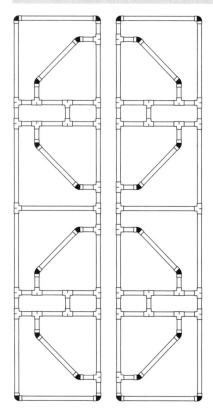

Octagon Panels

To show the effect of two "Octagon Panel" trellises placed next to each other.

Octagon Panels Combined

about 27"W x 54"H

Materials List

- 14 pipes cut to **d12**
- 8 pipes cut to **d9**
- 8 pipes cut to **d8.5(-)**
- 16 pipes cut to **d4.5**
- 46 pipes cut to **d3**
- 4 90° Elbow fittings
- 16 45° Elbow fittings
- 48 Tee fittings

Two Octagon Panels connected to each other with **d3** pipes. Assembly is as on the "Diagonals" trellis.

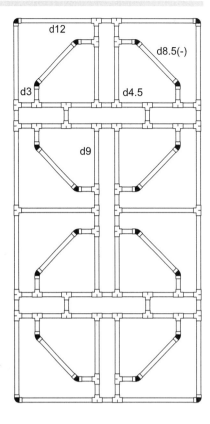

Octagon Arch Top

about 27"W x 51"H

This is the previous project with a few pipes at the top removed to expose an "arch".

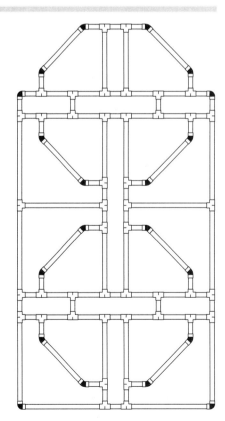

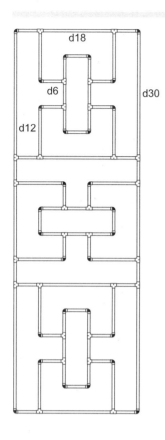

I-Beam

about 30"W x 90"H

Materials List

- 4 pipes cut to **d30**
- 6 pipes cut to **d18**
- 12 pipes cut to **d12**
- 48 pipes cut to **d6**
- 28 90° Elbow fittings
- 28 Tee fittings

Because of the long pipes, this trellis needs good support at top and bottom.

You can make this trellis in a shorter version by using just one or two of the repeating sections.

You can also make a 15"W x 45"H version of the entire design by substituting **d3** for **d6** pipes, **d6** for **d12** pipes, **d9** for **d18** pipes, and **d15** for **d30** pipes.

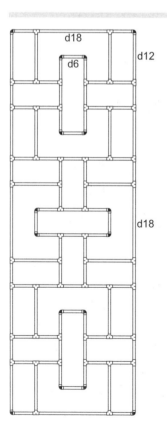

I-Beam Variation

about 30"W x 90"H

Materials List

- 4 pipes cut to **d18**
- 20 pipes cut to **d12**
- 70 pipes cut to **d6**
- 16 90° Elbow fittings
- 52 Tee fittings

This is a stronger version of the "I-Beam" because of shorter pipes and more Tee fittings.

As with the previous project, you can make fewer sections, or reduce the design by substituting pipes at half the listed size, **d3** instead of **d6** and so on.

You can also use one section of this project as a medallion for a wall or fence.

Snake

about 8"W x 72"H

Materials List

- 3 half inch pipes cut to **d17**
- 1 pipe cut to **d12**
- 1 pipe cut to **d8.5**
- 5 pipes cut to **d2.5**
- pipe for bending as given below
- 3 90° Elbow fittings
- 7 Tee fittings

Assembly Notes

This project may look difficult, but it is really quite simple. It consists of a straight pole with Tee fittings, and four bent pipes attached to the pole with more Tee fittings and "stubs". Bending the pipe is the only tricky part. It would be good to have some experience making simple bends with a conduit bender before attempting this project. This project is only for ½ inch copper pipe. The dimensions would be different for ¾ inch pipe because a conduit bender for ¾ inch pipe makes a different radius bend.

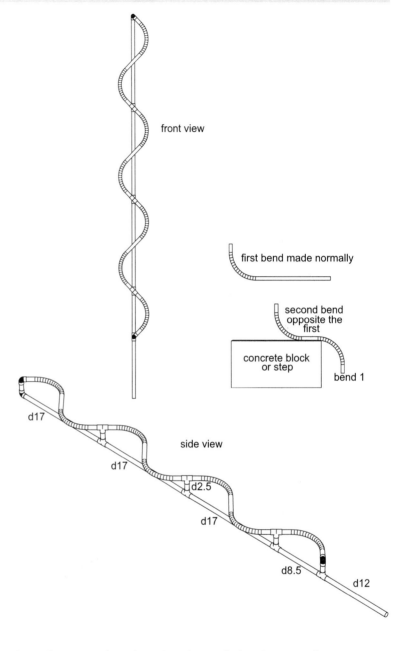

1. Start by assembling the entire straight pole with the Tee fittings and the **d2.5** pipes extending from the Tee fittings, but not the Tee fittings that will be used for the bent pipes. Use a jig or align the pole against long lengths of straight lumber on a flat table while assembling in order to make the pole as straight and unwarped as possible. The Tee fittings must all face in exactly the same direction.

2. Cut 3 pipes to 19-1/4" (actual dimension). Mark 1-1/8" from each end of each pipe. Put the start mark on your conduit bender directly over the marks on the pipes, and bend a 90° angle in each pipe. Then do the same at the other end of the pipes, but because you want an "S" shape and not a "U" shape, you make the second 90° bend point the opposite direction of the first bend. To do this you must put the first bend off the edge of some steps, a deck, or a concrete block. See the illustration.

3. When you make bends this close to the end of a pipe, the bender distorts the walls of the pipe a little bit. Check all the pipes and make sure they will accept Tee fittings. If they don't, use a pair of pliers to very gently squeeze the ends and return the pipe to a round shape. It only takes a slight amount of pressure with the pliers. (continued next page)

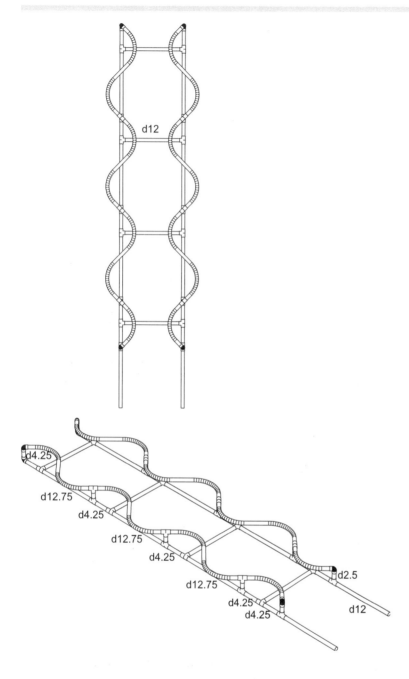

Waterfall

about 15"W x 72"H

The Waterfall is basically two "Snakes" from the previous project put together, with some extra pipe and fittings as shown. It would be good practice to make a Snake before attempting this project.

(Snake technique continued below)

4. Dry fit the 3 "S" pipes to the straight pole. If your bends are actually 90° and the bends are not warped or twisted in relation to each other, the "S" pipes should fit well. If the pipes do not fit well:

• Lay the bent pipe over the straight pole with fittings and check the length. The bent pipe should be just long enough to seat in the fittings at each end, and no more. Cut or file the ends if necessary.

• The angles in the "S" must be 90°. If not, the pipe will not enter the Tee fittings properly. Check the angles with a framing square if you have one, and adjust the bends to be as close to 90° as possible. If the pipes need more bend, you can turn over the conduit bender so the head is in the air and the handle is on the ground. Put the pipe back into the bender and push the pipe down around the bender. Be careful or you can go too far and start to crimp the pipe.

• Check that you made the bends in line with each other by sighting from an end of a bent pipe. If you see that one bend is tilted in relation to the other, it is best to bend a new "S" instead of attempting to force the warped pipe into position.

5. Assemble all the "S" pipes permanently.

6. The bent pipe at the bottom of the snake is an ordinary right angle bend. Make a right angle bend in a length of pipe, lay the pipe over the fittings, mark where to cut it so that 3/8" of pipe goes into the fitting at each end, and assemble it into the fittings.

Tall Narrow Fan

about 30"W x 106"H (Note: not a free standing design. Needs to be mounted to a fence or wall.)

Materials List

- 2 pieces ½ inch pipe cut to 106"
- 3 pieces ½ inch pipe cut to 87"
- 5 end caps
- 3 pieces 2x4 material, 30" long, 14" long, and 9-1/4" long

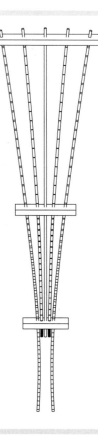

This project takes advantage of the natural flexibility of ½ inch diameter copper pipe. The pipe is not permanently bent. The spreader bars hold the pipe in a gentle curved shape. The spreader bars can be pressure treated wood or plastic lumber.

In the top spreader bar, drill 3/4" holes 6" on center, with 3" left at each end. In the middle spreader bar, drill 3/4" holes 2" on center, with 3" left at each end. In the bottom spreader bar, drill two 3/4" holes so the edges are 3" in from each end, then cut out the material between the holes so all 5 pipes fit next to each other in one slot.

Insert the pipes in the spreader bars, and fasten with brass screws into each pipe from the back of each spreader bar.

Short Fan

about 30"W x 48"H (Should be fastened to a wall or fence for support)

Materials List

- 7 pieces ½ inch hard copper pipe cut to 48"
- 2x4 material cut to 24", 15", and 10"
- 7 end caps

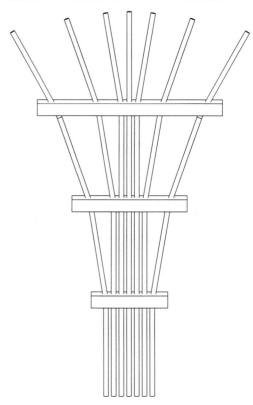

The center pipe in this project is straight. The two pipes on either side of center have a 10° bend 12" from the top. The next two pipes have 10° bends at 12" and 24" from the top. The outer pipes have 10° bends at 12", 24", and 36" from the top.

Bend the pipes first, then lay them next to each other in the pattern shown. Lay the 2x4 material over the bends, and mark where and at what angle to drill holes for the pipes. For the three center pipes in every spreader and all the holes in the bottom spreader, you can drill holes 11/16" in diameter and push the pipes in from the top. The other holes may need to be about 7/8" in diameter so you can insert the bent pipe.

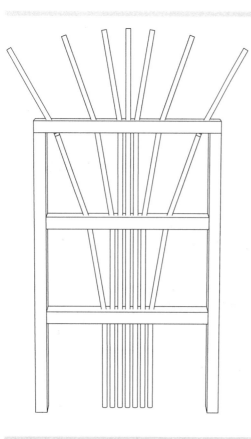

Fan with Wood Frame

This is the same as the previous project except the fan is supported inside a wood frame. The outer posts of this frame can be sunk in the ground to provide a free standing structure.

This design could be expanded to include several sections and make a "trellis fence" of whatever length you need.

If you use 2x4 lumber, the top horizontal piece is 24" wide. The two lower horizontal pieces are 21" wide. The outer posts are 36" long above ground. Be sure and make them longer if they will be sunk underground.

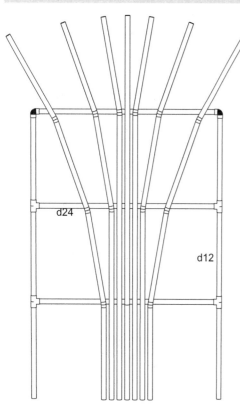

Fan with Pipe Frame

Materials List

The **extra** materials needed to build the pipe frame are:

- 3 pipes cut to **d24**
- 6 pipes cut to **d12**
- 2 90° Elbow fittings
- 4 Tee fittings

Make the lower legs longer than **d12** if they will be buried underground.

Fasten the trellis to the frame with brass screws from the back side.

Fan with Cross Bars

Materials List

The **extra** materials needed to build the cross bars are:

- 2 pipes cut to **d24**
- 2 pipes cut to **d15**
- 2 pipes cut to **d10**
- 6 pipes cut to 3/4"
- 12 90° Elbow fittings

All the cross bars are assembled as close to each other as possible by soldering a 3/4" length of pipe into an Elbow, and then soldering another Elbow over the part of the pipe sticking out. The joints of the Elbows will be touching.

Even then, the gap between the cross bars is wider than the pipes in the fan, so the cross bars are tilted as shown in order to contact the fan for maximum support.

Fasten with brass screws through the front and back of all cross bars.

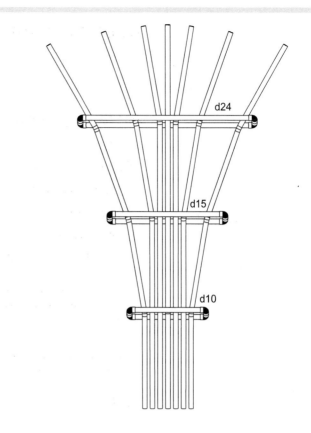

side view showing tilted cross bars

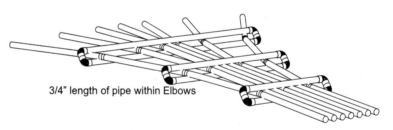

3/4" length of pipe within Elbows

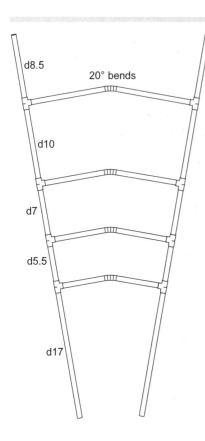

Bent Bar Fan

about 24"W x 48"H

Materials List

- 2 pipes cut to **d17** (or longer for underground support)
- 2 pipes cut to **d10**
- 2 pipes cut to **d8.5**
- 2 pipes cut to **d7**
- 2 pipes cut to **d5.5**
- 4 pipes about 24" long with a 20° bend in the middle
- 8 Tee fittings and 2 end caps

This project demonstrates how you can connect parts of a trellis at angles not provided for by standard fittings, by bending the cross bars instead.

In this case, the two sides of the fan are angled at 10° on either side of vertical, so the cross bars have 20° angles bent in them.

See below for assembly technique.

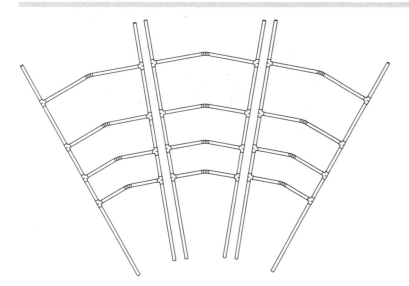

Spiderweb Fan

This is three of the Bent Bar Fans arranged together.

To assemble the basic Bent Bar Fan, start by assembling all the pipe and Tee fittings for each side of the fan.

Arrange the sides on the floor so that the tops are even (push them against a wall or straight board). Then angle the sides so the open ends of the top Tee fittings are 21" apart, and the open ends of the bottom Tee fittings are 12" apart.

Then bend 20° angles in the middle of four other pipes about 24" long. Lay the bent pipes over the Tee fittings, with the bends aligned down the center of the fan as shown. Mark where to cut the pipes, allowing 3/8" on each end of each pipe to go into the Tee fitting. Cut the pipes, dry fit to check if everything will fit properly, then put all the pieces together at once and solder the bent bars into the Tee fittings.

Woven Panel

about 24"W x 48"H

Materials List

- 12 pipes cut to **d12**
- 1 pipe cut to **d48**
- 3 pipes about 30" long bent as described below.
- 4 90° Elbow fittings
- 8 Tee fittings

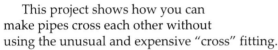

This project shows how you can make pipes cross each other without using the unusual and expensive "cross" fitting.

The crossover is accomplished by making a series of three bends in the center of each of the three long cross bars. The whole series of bends is referred to as a "saddle" by electricians.

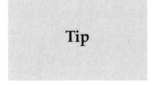 **Tip**	Making saddle bends takes practice. You may want to get a 10' piece of ½ inch electrical conduit, cut it into 30" pieces, and practice making saddle bends as described below. When you can get consistent results with the cheap conduit, then you can bend more expensive copper pipe the same way and not waste any copper pipe.

To make these saddle bends in ½ inch pipe with a ½ inch conduit bender:

1. Start with a pipe about 30" long. Make a mark 13" from one end. Using your bender in the normal manner with the pipe on the ground, bend a 45° angle starting with the start mark at the 13" mark and the heel of the bender towards the center of the pipe.

2. Mark the center of the bend you made. Then make two marks on the back side of the pipe 4-1/2" on either side of the center.

3. Turn your conduit bender so the head is in the air and the handle is on the ground. Put the pipe in the bender so one of the 4-1/2" marks you made is at the start mark. Push down on the pipe to bend it around the bending shoe until the bottom of the pipe contacts the bending groove near the 22° mark. Some conduit benders have sight lines built into the bending head for this type of "upside down" bending. If yours does, bend the pipe until the bottom lines up with the 22° sight line.

4. Put the other end of the pipe into the bender at the other 4-1/2" mark, and bend that pipe down to 22°. At this point you can sight down the pipe in the second bend and see when it is in line with the pipe on the other side of the 45° bend.

5. Now you can cut the bent pipes so the length from end to end is **d24**. **Important**: you must cut some pipe from both ends in order for the bend to be in the center of the cut pipe.

6. Dry fit the entire project with the bent pipes, and solder everything together.

CHAPTER 12

Arches and Arbors

In This Chapter

Arbors are popular garden structures, and can make strong supports for displaying large vines. An arch on top of two trellises is all you need to make an arbor. This chapter shows you lots of designs for making your own arches and arbors.

What is an Arbor?

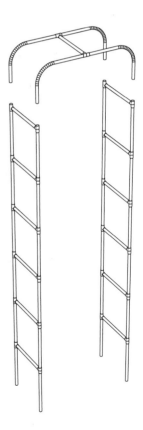

Think of an arbor as a combination of three structures: two uprights and one arch assembly, as shown in the illustration.

The uprights are simply flat trellises such as those shown in the previous chapter. Therefore, you can make an arbor by making two flat trellises and adding an arch top. The flat trellises can be any of the designs shown in the previous chapter, or a design of your own. For simplicity, most of the arbors in the illustrations in this chapter have uprights made from plain square type trellises.

Most of the trellis designs shown in the previous chapter have 90° Elbows at the top corners. To make a trellis so that it will accept an arch top, you simply make the trellis with Tee fittings at the top corners instead of the Elbows.

The width of the opening through an arbor has nothing to do with the uprights or trellises you use to make it. The width of the opening is determined by the span of the arch you make. So if you make a three foot arch for instance, and later decide that the opening is too narrow, you could either replace the arch with a longer one, or possibly cut the existing one and add more Tee fittings and pipe to lengthen the span. You wouldn't need to rebuild the entire arbor.

Before You Begin

Before you design and build an arbor, ask yourself these questions:

- Do you have space for an arbor?

- Is the arbor just a decoration, or will people walk through it or sit under it?

- Will people walk through it daily, or only occasionally?

- Does the arbor need to fill a certain space?

- What kind of plants do you want to grow on the arbor?

- Will an arbor provide an interesting focal point?

- Will an arbor hide something you would rather be able to view?

- Can you use an arbor to hide something you don't want to view?

Practical Considerations

Assuming you have decided that you have a good space for an arbor and want to make one, here are some things you should think about that affect the size of the arbor:

- If your arbor is purely a decorative plant support, and people do not need to walk through it, you can make the arbor any size you want. You can make tiny or child size arbors, or tall narrow arbors similar to an obelisk or pillar.

- If people are going to walk through an arbor, a three foot wide arbor is the bare minimum. This is because the type of plants that quickly cover an arbor aren't going to just grow upwards, they are also going to extend into the interior of the arbor. If you grow a naturally bushy plant or get behind in your pruning and stems grow in six inches from each side of the arbor, that would leave only a two foot space for people to pass through without brushing the plants. That might be OK if the plant on the arbor is a fragrant honeysuckle, but certainly not a rose.

- In the same way, if you intend to have an arbor large enough to have a bench so you can sit under the arbor, the width of the arbor will have to be at least the width of the bench, plus space for plant growth.

- Consider the height of the arbor in the same way. Will people be able to walk through it without brushing their heads on plants?

- An easy way to get a feel for the minimum size a people-arbor should be is to look at the doorways in your house - they are designed for people to walk through comfortably. Your arbor should probably be large enough so that with plants growing on both sides and the top, you still have a nice "doorway".

- Normally you grow plants on an arbor, and the arbor must be able to support the weight of the plant and the force of the wind blowing against the plant. Light annual vines can use lightweight arbors made from ½ inch diameter pipe. Large, heavy, leafy vines require strongly built arbors made from ¾ inch diameter pipe.

About Making Arches

There are two basic ways you can make an arch top for an arbor. One is by assembling straight pipes with fittings, the other is by bending.

If you assemble an arch top with straight pipe and fittings, the basic building blocks of the arch will always be some sort of rectangular assemblies. You can assemble these parts flat on a table or by using an assembly jig as shown in **"Measuring Jigs, Assembly Jigs, and Clamping"** on page 27. Then the rectangular sub assemblies can be assembled to each other with 90° or 45° Elbow fittings.

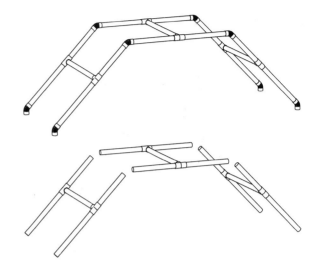

In the arch shown in the illustration, the straight pipes and fittings that make up the "H" shapes can be assembled flat on a table or jig. 45° Elbow fittings are added between the sub assemblies to complete the arch.

To make an arch by bending, the best way to get accurate results is to first bend the complete arch shape you want in two separate pipes. Make sure that the two bent pipes are as identical as possible. Then cut the pipes apart at the exact same spots and insert Tee fittings and cross bars.

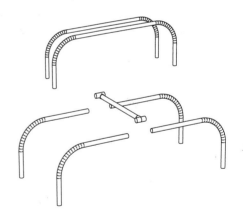

For the best strength and stability in your completed arbor, try to put cross bars in your arches at 12 to 18" intervals.

More information about bending arches is in **"How to Bend Copper Pipe"** on page 41.

More information about assembling arches from bent pipe is under the heading **"Using your arches in an arbor"** on page 60.

Most of the arch styles with bends are illustrated as if the bends were made by using hard copper pipe and a conduit bender. You can get similar results by bending soft copper tube with the aid of bending jigs.

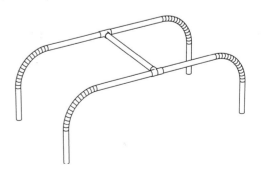

Hard copper pipe will make a more rigid arbor. Remember that soft copper tube will bend just as easily when it is part of an arbor or trellis as it will in your hands. Use soft copper tube only for supporting lightweight vines, and arbors that will not be subjected to a lot of stress.

Peak Top Arch

Materials List

- 8 pipes cut to **dx**, from table below
- 2 pipes for the cross bars, cut to the same length as the cross bars in your uprights
- 2 90° Elbow fittings
- 4 45° Elbow fittings
- 4 Tee fittings

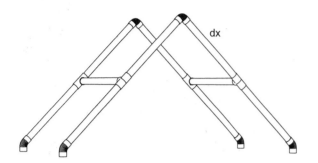

Arch span (opening)	dx	Height of arch
24"	d8.5	12"
36"	d12.75	18"
48"	d17	24"

Large Peak Top Arch

Materials List

- 12 pipes cut to **dx**, from the table below
- 4 pipes for the cross bars, cut to the same length as the cross bars in your uprights.
- 2 90° Elbow fittings
- 4 45° Elbow fittings
- 8 Tee fittings

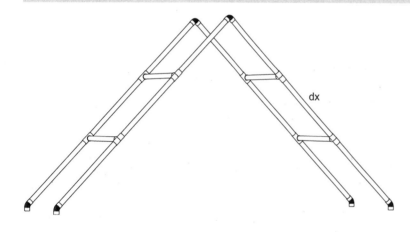

Arch span (opening)	dx	Height of arch
48"	d11-5/16	24"
60"	d14-1/8	30"
72"	d17	36"

Large Peak Top Arch with Cross Bracing

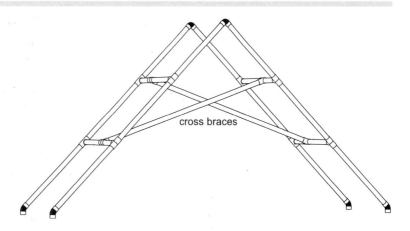

This arch is the same as the large peak top arch on the previous page, but with modified cross bars and the addition of two cross braces. The best assembly technique is different from usual though.

1. For this arch, instead of assembling the rectangular parts on a table or with a jig, start by assembling the two large "L" shapes. The "L" shapes are all the parts except cross bars and cross braces. You **do** want to put the Tee fittings and Elbows in the positions shown.

2. After you have the two "L" shapes, lay them flat on a floor. Make sure they have the dimension you want. If they are supposed to be spanning 48", make sure the measurement across the open ends of the "L" is 48" center-to-center. If the legs are a little bit off, hold them to the dimension they should have with weights such as concrete blocks.

3. Now measure across the centers of the Tee fittings that will be holding the cross braces, in the same way that the cross braces will go – from the Tee fitting for the top cross bar on one side to Tee fitting for the bottom cross bar on the other side.

4. Since that is a center-to-center measurement, the length of the cross braces will be 3/4" less if using ½ inch diameter pipe, and 1" less if using ¾ inch diameter pipe. Cut pipe for the two cross braces and put a Tee fitting at each end.

5. So the cross braces won't interfere with each other, cut pipes to make cross bars at one-third and two-thirds of the cross bar's total length. For instance, if the cross bars in the arbor uprights were made to **d12**, you would cut the pipes for the arch cross bars to **d4** and **d8**.

6. Now assemble the cross bar pipes into the cross brace Tee fittings, making sure the same size pipes are on the same side of the cross brace Tee fittings. For instance, both **d4** pipes on one side, and both **d8** pipes on the other side.

7. Finally, assemble the cross braces with cross bars into the "L" shapes. You will need to assemble the cross braces into the arch so one cross brace is closer to one side of the arch, and the other cross brace is closer to the other side of the arch.

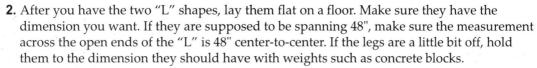

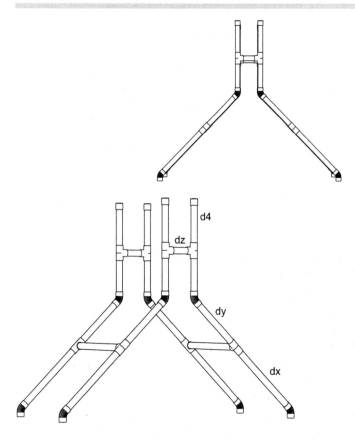

Peak Top Arch with Open Finial

Materials List

- 4 pipes cut to **dx**, from table below
- 4 pipes cut to **dy**, from table below
- 8 pipes cut to **d4**
- 2 pipes cut to **dz**, see notes
- 2 pipes cut for cross bars, to match the cross bars in your uprights
- 8 45° Elbow fittings,8 Tee fittings, 4 end caps

Arch span	dx	dy
24"	d8.5	d5.5
36"	d12.75	d9.75
48"	d17	d14

Dimension **dz** should be about **d4.25**, but cut these pipes last and dry fit the two halves of the arch so that the arch has the span you want.

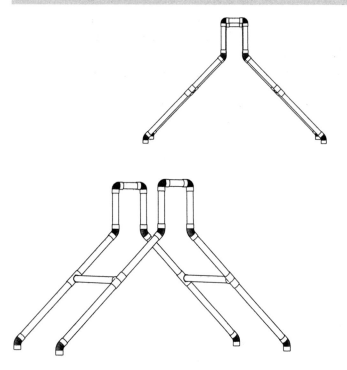

Peak Top Arch with Closed Finial

This is the same as the project above, except it does not use the top two pipes that make the open finial, and it uses Elbows instead of Tee Fittings to close off the top.

All the dimensions are the same as above.

High Arch with 45° Elbows

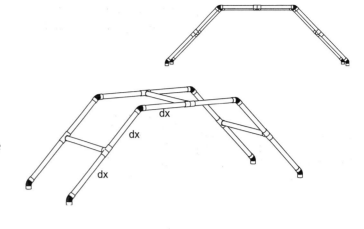

Materials List

- 12 pipes cut to **dx**, from table below
- 3 pipes cut for cross bars, to match the cross bars in your uprights
- 8 45° Elbow fittings, 6 Tee fittings

Arch span	dx	Height of arch
~24"	d5	7"
~36"	d7-1/2	10.5"
~48"	d10	14"

The dimensions given for **dx** will give the approximate arch span shown. Fit your uprights to the arch you make, don't try to make the arch fit an exact distance between uprights.

Shallow Arch with 45° Elbows

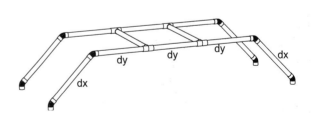

Materials List

- 4 pipes cut to **dx**, from table below
- 6 pipes cut to **dy**, from table below
- 2 pipes cut for cross bars, to match the cross bars in your uprights
- 8 45° Elbow fittings, 4 Tee fittings

Again, the dimensions given for **dx** and **dy** will give the approximate arch span shown.

Arch span	dx	dy	Height of arch
~24"	d6-3/8	d5	4.5"
~36"	d8-1/2	d8	6"
~48"	d10-5/8	d11	7.5"
~60"	d14-3-4	d13	10.5"

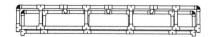

Modern Flat Top Arch

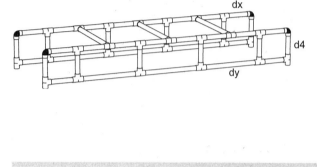

Materials List

- 6 pipes cut to **dx**, from the table below

- 20 pipes cut to **dy**, from the table below

- 12 pipes cut to **d4**

- 3 pipes cut for cross bars, to match the cross bars in your uprights

- 4 90° Elbow fittings

- 26 Tee fittings

Modern Flat Top Arbor

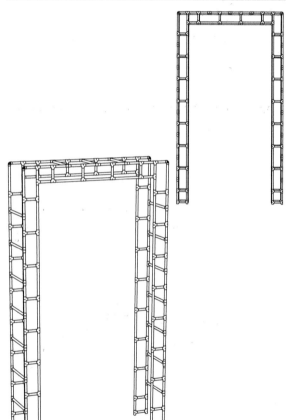

The uprights shown are made from the same dimension pipes as the flat top, but with more "middle" sections to make the uprights as tall as you want.

Examine the Tee fittings and pipes in the top corners of the illustration and you will be able to see the modifications you need to build in if you want to assemble this style top to this style of uprights.

Pipe dimensions for the top:

Arch span	dx	dy
24"	d3	d6
36"	d4.5	d9
48"	d6	d12
60"	d7.5	d15

For the uprights, you can use the dimensions as if you were making a top to span 60". Adding one more middle section would increase the arbor height to 75", adding two more middle sections would increase the arbor height to 90", and so on.

You can "mix and match" pipe sizes for the middle sections from the table above to arrive at the exact height you want.

Basic Bent Arbor

MINIATURE VERSION

This is a very simple miniature arbor you can make by bending a circular arch in the center of a full 10' piece of pipe.

To make a reasonably smooth circular arch like this you will need to use the arch bending jig as shown on page 51.

The arch is made from eighteen 10° bends. The width of the opening you want determines the spacing between bends, and is given in the table on page 53.

The table below shows how far from one end of the pipe to start making your bends so that the arch will come out in the center of a 10' piece of pipe, and how tall the finished arbor will be.

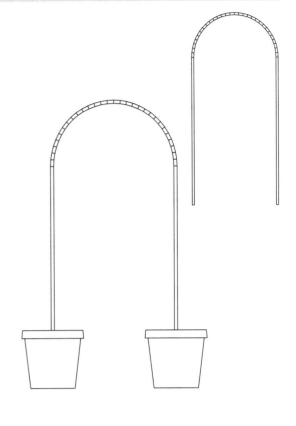

Arch span (opening)	Start Bending at	Height of arbor
24"	41"	53"
36"	32"	50"
48"	22"	46"
60"	13"	43"

The first two arbors in the table will look like arbors, with long legs. The second two arbors will look more like giant row cover support hoops (and could be used as such if you wanted).

All dimensions are approximate, and the accuracy of your bending jig and your own bending style will also affect the results. You will probably need to trim a little extra pipe off one of the arbor legs and/or carefully adjust your bends to make the arch come out looking even.

FULL SIZE VERSION

If you want a full size arbor big enough to walk through, you can use couplings and add straight legs to the arbors. For instance, if you want a 36" wide, 80" tall arbor, you can add 30" legs to the arbor with the 36" opening from the table above. (80" height wanted minus 50" height of the arbor as made from 10' pipe equals 30" more height needed.)

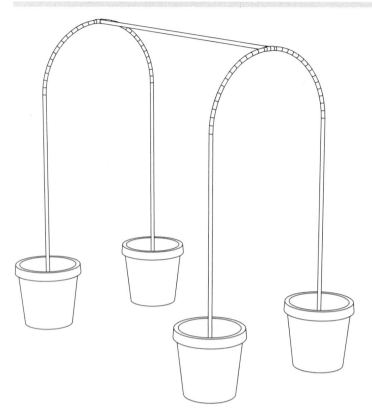

Walkway from Basic Bent Arbors

Instead of putting an entire circular arch in the middle of a 10' piece of pipe and then adding additional legs, you can get the same results by making half of an arbor in two separate pipes, and then joining the pipes together at the top center.

To make half an arch, use the arch bending jig, starting right at the end of a 10' length of pipe.

Make nine 10° bends instead of eighteen, using the spacing between bends that will give you the arch span or opening that you want, as shown in the table on page 53.

Then do the same with another pipe. Join the arch halves at the top with a coupling if you want a single arch.

If you want to connect two arbors and make a walkway as shown in the illustration, use Tee fittings at the top center and use straight pipe to connect the two simple arbors.

Finally, cut the straight legs to whatever length you want, remembering to leave extra if the legs will be buried in the ground for support.

This lightweight arbor would be suitable for supporting lightweight annual plants such as Morning Glories or Cardinal Climber. You can add plastic coated wire fencing to the sides for extra support for the plants if you wish.

Flat Top Arch by Bending

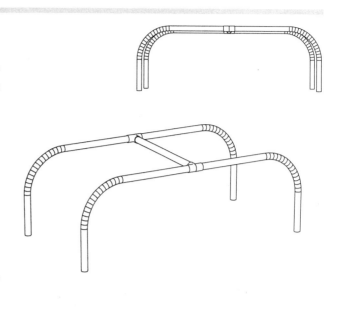

Put 90° bends in two pipes, so the center-to-center distance between the ends of each pipe is equal to the span of the arch you want.

The complete procedure for making bends like this is given on page 45.

After bending the pipes, align the pipes next to each other, mark the center on both pipes, cut the pipes at the mark, and assemble a cross bar with Tee fittings to connect the parts.

Because a Tee fitting takes up space, your arch will turn out a little wider than the span shown in the table below. Or you can cut a little extra off the arch pipes to arrive at the exact span you want.

The cross bar is the same size as the cross bars in your uprights.

The dimensions shown will result in 3" vertical legs on the ends of the arch, similar to the illustration. If you want longer legs, start with a longer piece of pipe. You still put the start marks the same distance apart, centered within the length of pipe.

Arch span	Length of pipe before bending	Start marks this far apart
~24"	36"	30", or 3" from each end
~36"	48"	42", or 3" from each end
~48"	60"	54", or 3" from each end
~60"	72"	66", or 3" from each end

Tip	This arch used by itself would make a good row cover support. Make the size that will span your garden bed, and make the cross bar as long as you want.

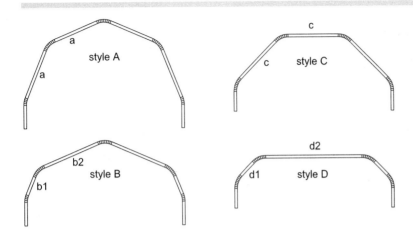

Arch Styles Based on 45° Bends

All arches shown start and end with a short length of vertical pipe.

The tables show the distance between the **centers** of the bends.

To put a 45° bend at a certain center point, you must put your start mark 2" away from the center, when using ½ inch diameter copper pipe and a ½ inch conduit bender.

To put a 22.5° bend at a certain center point, you must put your start mark 1" away from the center.

See **"How to position the bends for common angles"** on page 47.

Styles **A** and **B** have bends 22.5°, 3x45°, 22.5°.

Arch span	a	b1	b2
~24"	9-3/16"	4.5"	11-1/8"
~36"	13-3/4"	7"	16-5/8"
~48"	18-3/8"	9"	22-1/4"
~60"	23"	11.5"	27-3/4"

Styles **C** and **D** have bends 4x45°.

Arch span	c	d1	d2
~24"	10"	5"	17"
~36"	15"	7.5"	25-3/8"
~48"	20"	10"	33-3/4"
~60"	25"	12.5"	42-1/4"

Arch Styles Based on 60° Bends

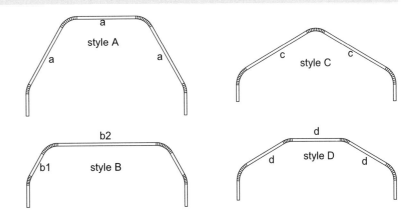

style A

style C

style B

style D

All arches shown start and end with a short length of vertical pipe.

The tables show the distance between the **centers** of the bends.

To put a 60° bend at a certain center point, you must put your start mark 2-5/8" away from the center, when using ½ inch diameter copper pipe and a ½ inch conduit bender.

To put a 30° bend at a certain center point, you must put your start mark 1-1/4" away from the center.

See **"How to position the bends for common angles"** on page 47.

Styles **A** and **B** have bends 30°, 2x60°, 30°.

Arch span	a	b1	b2
~24"	12"	6"	18"
~36"	18"	9"	27"
~48"	24"	12"	36"
~60"	30"	15"	45"

Style **C** has bends 3x60°. Style **D** has bends 60°, 2x30°, 60°

Arch span	c	d
~24"	13-7/8"	8-3/4"
~36"	20-3/4"	13-3/16"
~48"	27-3/4"	17-5/8"
~60"	34-5/8"	22"

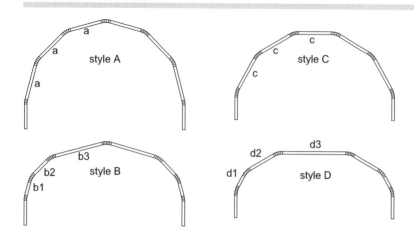

Arch Styles Based on 30° Bends

All arches shown start and end with a short length of vertical pipe.

The tables show the distance between the **centers** of the bends.

To put a 30° bend at a certain center point, you must put your start mark 1-1/4" away from the center, when using ½ inch diameter copper pipe and a ½ inch conduit bender.

To put a 15° bend at a certain center point, you must put your start mark 5/8" away from the center. Conduit benders do not have 15° marks. You can add your own about halfway between the 10° and 22° marks.

See **"How to position the bends for common angles"** on page 47.

Styles **A** and **B** have bends 15°, 5x30°, 15°.

Arch span	a	b1	b2	b3
~24"	6-1/4"	3-1/8"	4-1/4"	8-3/4"
~36"	9-5/16"	4-5/8"	6-7/16"	13"
~48"	12-7/16"	6-1/4"	8-1/2"	17-3/8"
~60"	15-1/2"	7-3/4"	10-5/8"	21-3/4"

Styles **C** and **D** have bends 6x30°.

Arch span	c	d1	d2	d3
~24"	6-7/16"	3-1/4"	5-5/8"	11-1/8"
~36"	9-5/8"	4-3/4"	8-3/8"	16-3/4"
~48"	12-7/8"	6-7/16"	11-3/16"	22-3/8"
~60"	16"	8"	14"	28"

Arbors with Arch Tops by Bending

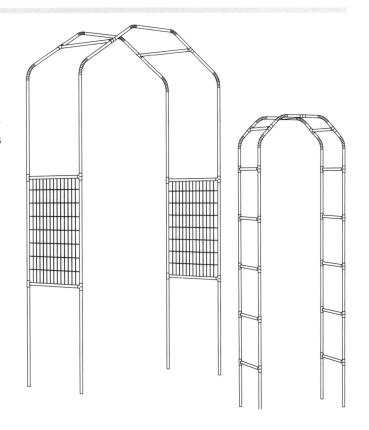

The illustrations show some examples of how arch tops made by bending might look in place as part of an arbor, complete with cross bars.

To the right are two different size arbors. The arbor on the left has a "style D" arch from page 121. The arbor on the right has a "style C" arch from page 120.

The large arbor serves as a reminder that you can use plastic mesh fencing material in the openings of your arbor if you want to grow plants that require more support than the frame of your arbor provides.

On the left below is another size arbor made from a "style D" arch on page 121, and on the right an arbor made from a "style A" arch from page 120.

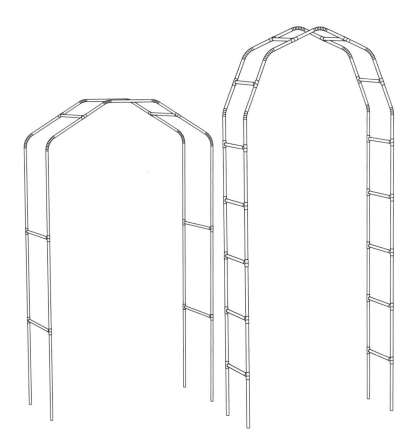

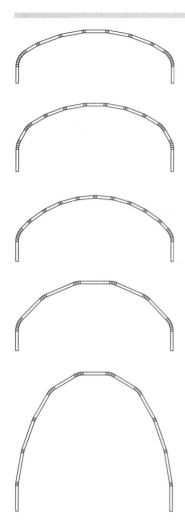

Arch Styles Based on Ellipses

The arch styles shown in the illustration were developed to allow you to approximate an elliptical arch by making a series of evenly spaced bends at different angles.

More information about these arches is under the heading **"Elliptical arch styles you can bend from hard copper pipe"** on page 56.

CHAPTER 13

Obelisks, Pillars, and Spirals

In This Chapter

Obelisks and pillars are popular garden ornaments for supporting climbing plants. The spiral is a popular topiary shape. By using a spiral frame you can train most any plant into a spiral topiary.

How an Obelisk differs from a Trellis

Most trellises are more or less flat, and can be used to screen off or define a space as well as support plants. Many trellises can be mounted against a fence or wall, whereas an obelisk or pillar is usually a free standing structure with three or more legs, and is usually used as a decoration, focal point, or garden accent. An obelisk can be more stable than a trellis because it has more legs for support and is usually shorter.

An obelisk is typically three to five feet tall. You can see over and around a typical obelisk, where a full size trellis might block your view. An obelisk can be used to support most any kind of vine or climbing plant. Many vines will quickly reach the top of an obelisk and tumble back down. If you choose a fast growing leafy vine, your obelisk may soon be completely obscured by the plant and give the effect of a tall bush. If you choose a smaller leafed vine such as cardinal climber, you will be able to see the obelisk as well as the plant.

Gardeners refer to many types of free standing structures as obelisks, pillars, or even "tuteurs". A pillar usually has a columnar shape. An obelisk usually has a pointed top, like the Washington Monument.

Before you Begin

Most of the projects in this chapter are illustrated as they would appear above ground. If you will be supporting the obelisk or pillar by burying some pipe, be sure to lengthen the legs by 12-18". In addition to the projects shown in this chapter, be sure to look at the "pot trellis" projects in the Trellis Designs chapter. If you enlarge most any of the pot trellis designs, you will have a simple pillar. And if you scale down some of the designs shown in this chapter, you can make some fancier pot trellises.

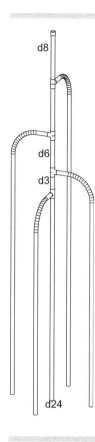

Waterfall Pillar about 18"W x 49"H

Materials List

- 1 each copper pipe cut to **d3** and **d6**
- 2 pipes cut to **d8**
- 1 pipe cut to **d24**
- 4 pipes with 90° bends
- 4 Tee fittings, 1 end cap

This is the same as the Waterfall trellis project in the Trellis Designs chapter on page 80, but with the legs rotated around the central pole.

Make the central pole first, with the Tee fittings facing in the directions shown. Then, instead of trying to bend pipes with exact measurements, just make four pipes with 90° bends and arrange them next to the fittings on the central pole in a way that you like. Then mark where to make the cuts, cut the pipes and assemble the bent pipes into the Tee fittings. Last, cut the legs to the same length, leaving extra for underground support if needed.

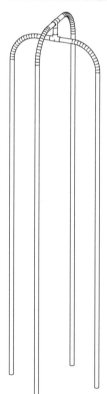

Arch Top Pillar

about 12"W x 48"H

Materials List

- 2 pipes with two 90° bends as shown
- 1 pipe cut to **d3**
- 2 Tee fittings

You can make this pillar whatever size you want by using longer or shorter pipes and placing the 90° bends closer or further apart. For an approximately 4' tall by 1' wide pillar, start with 10' pieces of pipe and place bends in the middle centered 12" apart.

See page 44 for how to make 90° bends like this. After you make bends in two pipes, cut the pipes at the top center, insert a Tee fitting to reconnect the two halves, and then connect the two arches with the short **d3** pipe. Finally, cut the legs to the same length, or leave as is and bury part of the legs underground for support.

This project doesn't use any cross bars, so to keep the legs in a fixed position you need to use rebar supports or put part of the legs underground.

Arch Top Pillar with Cross Bars

about 12"W x 54"H

Materials List

- 2 pipes with two 90° bends as shown
- 4 pipes cut to **d12** (see below)
- 1 pipe cut to **d3**
- 10 Tee fittings

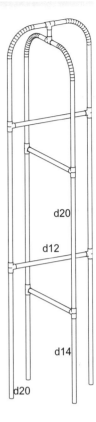

See the previous project for more assembly technique. You can bend two long pipes, then cut them where the cross bars will go at approximately **d14** and **d20** as shown, add tees, and reconnect the legs and cross bars.

The **d12** cross bar dimension is just a guideline. You should cut the cross bars after you have made your bends and reconnected the arches. Then you can get the exact dimension for the cross bars to fit the bends you made.

Cross Bar Pillar with Wire

This is a reminder that you can add wire or plastic fencing to any project you make to provide extra support for plants that need it, or as a decorative element. The wire can be instead of or in addition to copper pipe cross bars.

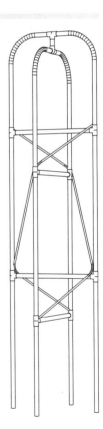

You can make geometric or artistic designs by bending bare copper electrical wire. Bare copper electrical wire is available in the electrical department at the home centers. They can cut wire to any length you want from a large spool. They typically have "6 gauge" wire, which is very thick wire, about 11/32" diameter, and "4 gauge" wire, which is even thicker, about 7/32" diameter.

You can wrap the wire around the pipes, insert it in holes in the pipes, or solder it permanently using the same techniques as when soldering copper pipe (clean, flux, and solder).

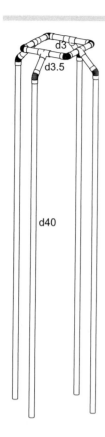

Square Top Obelisk

about 10"W x 42"H

Materials List

- 4 pipes cut to **d40**
- 4 pipes cut to **d3.5**
- 8 pipes cut to **d3**
- 4 90° Elbow fittings
- 4 45° Elbow fittings
- 4 Tee fittings

None of the dimensions for this project are critical.

You can make the top larger by using **d4** or **d6** pipes to form the square instead of **d3**.

You can make the whole obelisk wider by using **d6** or longer pipes instead of the **d3.5**.

You can make the obelisk taller or shorter by using some other pipe size than **d40** for the legs.

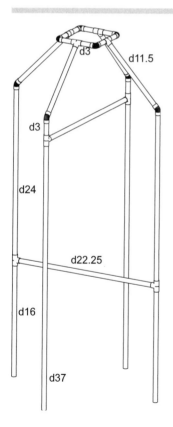

Large Square Top Obelisk

about 23"W x 52"H

Materials List

- 2 pipes cut to **d37**
- 2 pipes cut to **d24**
- 2 pipes cut to **d22.25** (see below)
- 2 pipes cut to **d16**
- 2 pipes cut to **d11.5**
- 10 pipes cut to **d3**
- 4 90° Elbow fittings
- 4 45° Elbow fittings
- 8 Tee fittings

The **d22.5** cross bars are shown as a guideline. Assemble the square top first, then the angled pipes, then you can determine the exact dimension for the cross bars from your actual construction.

Large Square Top Obelisk with Cross Bars about 16"W x 54"H

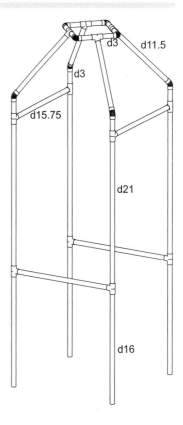

Materials List

- 4 pipes cut to **d21**
- 4 pipes cut to **d16**
- 4 pipes cut to **d15.75**
- 4 pipes cut to **d11.5**
- 12 pipes cut to **d3**
- 4 90° Elbow fittings
- 4 45° Elbow fittings
- 12 Tee fittings

See the previous projects for assembly techniques.

Large Square Top Obelisk by Bending

about 16"W x 54"H

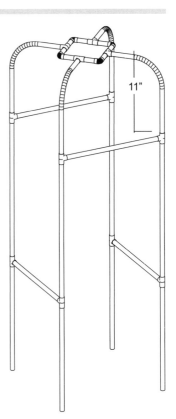

This project is the same as the previous, but with bent pipes replacing the 45° Elbow fittings and angled pipes.

The Tee fittings in the top square are facing horizontally, not angled down.

The easy way to make the bent top is to make 90° bends in the middle of pipes about 30" long. Cut off one leg on all the pipes to about 11" long from the top of the bent pipe to the bottom of the vertical pipe as shown in the illustration. Dry fit the bent pipes in place on the frame, using clamps if necessary. Assemble the top square, lay it over the bent pipes, and mark where to cut the pipes. Remember to allow extra pipe to go into the Tee fittings in the top square - 3/8" in the case of ½ inch diameter pipe.

After cutting, dry fit the whole top to check for any problems, then assemble the square top to the bent pipes and the bent pipes to the main frame.

You can also form the bends from soft copper tube, either freehand or by using a simple jig.

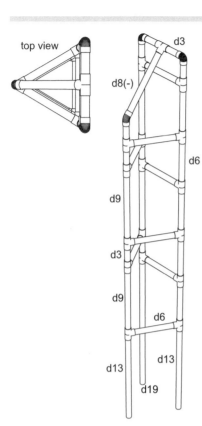

Angled Top Obelisk

about 8"W x 46"H

Materials List

- 1 pipe cut to **d19**, 2 pipes cut to **d13** (lower legs)
- 4 pipes cut to **d9** (verticals in two of the legs)
- 1 pipe cut to **d8(-)** (angled top)
- 13 pipes cut to **d6** (all cross bars, and verticals in one leg)
- 9 pipes cut to **d3** (all the smallest pipes shown)
- 2 90° Elbow fittings
- 1 45° Elbow fitting
- 17 Tee fittings

Most of this project is straightforward. Assemble the three legs working from the bottom up. When you get to the angled top, do a dry fit of the angled piece. The **d8(-)** dimension means the angled pipe should be slightly less than **d8**, but you can make whatever adjustments you need when you dry fit.

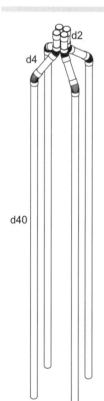

Four Legged Obelisk

about 8"W x 46"H

Materials List

- 4 pipes cut to **d40**
- 4 pipes cut to **d4**
- 4 pipes cut to **d2**
- 8 45° Elbow fittings
- 4 end caps

Everything about this project is adjustable.

Change the **d40** pipes to make the obelisk taller or shorter. Change the **d4** pipes to make the obelisk wider. Change the **d2** pipes to make a longer finial.

The top pipes at the finial can be wrapped together with copper wire or fastened with brass screws. To keep the legs in position, the legs should be either sunk in the ground or supported by rebar within. As usual, allow extra length for the legs if you will be putting them in the ground.

Open Top Obelisk about 8"W x 32"H

Materials List

- 2 pipes cut to **d12.5** (longer verticals in two legs)
- 1 pipe cut to **d10** (long vertical in one leg)
- 6 pipes cut to **d8** (all cross bars)
- 2 pipes cut to **d5.5** (parts in two legs); 2 pipes cut to **d5** (parts in one leg)
- 7 pipes cut to **d3** (parts in legs and the angled top)
- 7 pipes cut to **d2.5** (parts in legs and the angled top)
- 6 45° Elbow fittings, 12 Tee fittings, 3 end caps

There is nothing too difficult about this project even though the multiple parts for the legs look complicated.

To make sure you are getting the right lengths, check the illustration for which legs attach at the same fitting height and make sure the lengths add up. At the bottom of this obelisk for instance, the **d3** and **d2.5** legs equal the **d5.5** leg. The **d5.5** and **d2.5** legs equal the **d3** and **d5** legs.

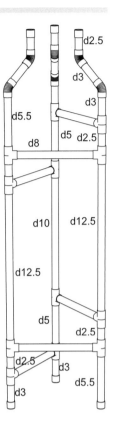

Open and Closed Top Obelisk Variations

about 8"W x 32"H

These are basically the same as the previous project.

In the first variation the open angled top is made by bending either hard pipe or soft copper tube.

In the next variation the top is closed. Most materials are the same as the "Open Top Obelisk" except for 3 pipes cut to **d6** to make the angled top.

In the third variation the closed angled top is also made by bending either hard pipe or soft copper tube.

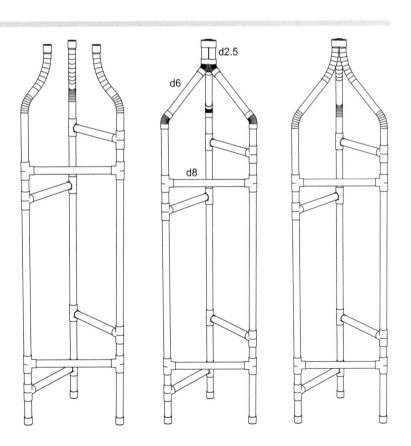

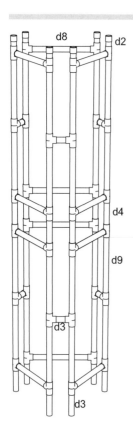

Three Sided Pillar

about 12"W x 45"H

Materials List

- 24 pipes cut to **d9** (longer pipes in the legs)
- 12 pipes cut to **d8** (long cross bars)
- 6 pipes cut to **d4** (middle pipes in legs)
- 12 pipes cut to **d3** (bottom ends of legs and short cross bars)
- 6 pipes cut to **d2** (tops of legs)
- 36 Tee fittings, 6 end caps

One way to assemble a project such as this is to work from the bottom up. Assemble two "levels" of pipe but only solder the fittings in the lower level. The upper level is clamped in position and acts as an "assembly helper" to keep the lower level in alignment.

Then add another level of pipes but solder the level below that, and so on until you get to the top.

You can increase the length of the **d3** cross bars if you wish to make a wider pillar. If you change them to **d8** you will get an open hexagon shape.

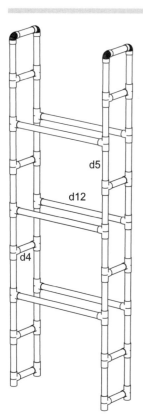

Modern Pillar

about 12"W x 40"H

Materials List

- 6 pipes cut to **d12** (long cross bars)
- 32 pipes cut to **d5** (all verticals)
- 12 pipes cut to **d4** (short cross bars)
- 4 90° Elbow fittings
- 32 Tee fittings

This project is easiest to make by assembling each of the two sides on a flat table, paying attention to face the Tee fittings for the cross bars in the right direction. Then stand the sides up and assemble the **d12** cross bars between the two sides.

Make the **d4** cross bars longer if you want a wider pillar. If you make them **d12** you will have a very open square shape.

Bent Bar Obelisk

about 26"W x 40"H

Materials List

- 4 pipes cut to **d10**
- 4 pipes cut to **d8.5**
- 4 pipes cut to **d7**
- 4 pipes cut to **d5.5**
- 4 pipes cut to **d4.25**
- 8 pipes with 20° bends in the middle for the cross bars
- 2 pipes with 70° bends in the middle for the top arches.
- 4 45° Elbow fittings
- 16 Tee fittings

This project is almost exactly like the "Bent Bar Fan" trellis project on page 106, except two of the "Bent Bar Fans" are angled towards each other and connected. The main difference is that some of the Tee fittings face in different directions. See that project for assembly and fitting technique.

The top arch of this project can be made by bending soft copper tube or hard copper pipe.

You need a 70° angle in the hard copper pipe, which is not an angle marked on conduit benders. You can bend to the 60° mark and then estimate another 10°. Make one and dry fit it to the frame, then bend another that matches it.

You can make minor adjustments to an already-bent piece of hard copper pipe by closing one end of the pipe with tape and filling the pipe with dry sand. Tap the pipe on a table to settle the sand and keep adding more until the pipe is filled. Tape off the remaining end, and then bend by hand or with the help of a vise. The sand will help prevent the pipe from collapsing or kinking.

You can form soft copper tube around a jig to the exact shape of the arch shown, or you can bend tube by hand to any sort of arch that fits between the top fittings.

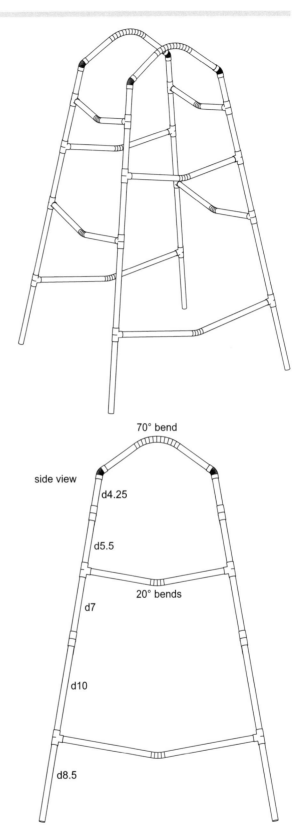

70° bend

side view

d4.25

d5.5

20° bends

d7

d10

d8.5

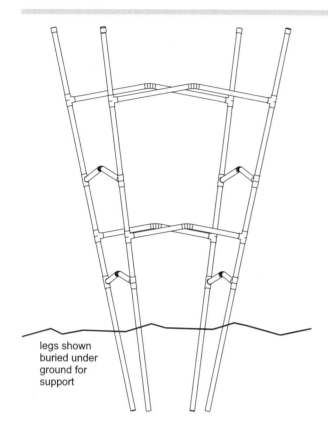

legs shown
buried under
ground for
support

Bent Bar Four Sided Fan

about 26"W x 40"H above ground

This is the same as the previous project, except:

- turned upside down
- no top arches
- longer pipes to enable support by sinking
the pipes underground
- end caps on the pipes above ground

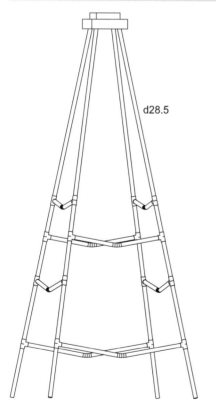

d28.5

Tuteur about 26"W x 60"H

Materials List

- Same as for the "Bent Bar Obelisk" except the **d4.25** pipes are
replaced by **d28.5** pipes.
- Wood, plastic wood, or ready-made finial for top

You can increase the length of the **d28.5** pipes if you wish. As shown,
they will allow the use of a finial about 6" square or round. If you
increase them to **d32.5** you can use a smaller finial. If you increase them
to **d36.5** they will meet and form a pyramid top.

d36.5

Spiral from Copper Tube

about 15"W x 48"H

Materials List

- 1 10′ coil of ½ inch diameter soft copper tube
- 8 ½ inch diameter hard copper pipes cut to **d6** (for all the verticals in the center pole)
- 8 ½ inch pipes to make the spokes, cut to the actual dimensions shown with the center pole illustration
- 3 90° Elbow fittings
- 13 Tee fittings

This project may look complicated, but actually it is pretty easy. It takes advantage of the fact that soft copper tube is supplied as a coil. All you are going to do is cut the coil apart and rearrange the pieces around a center pole. Here is the complete procedure:

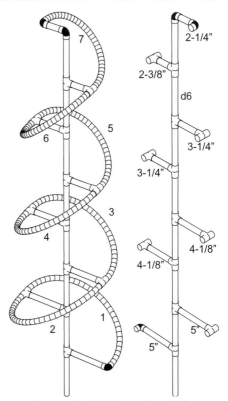

make lowest vertical longer than d6 if you want to sink part of the pole underground

1. Cut hard copper pipe to the dimensions shown and assemble the complete center pole. The verticals are all **d6**. For the spokes, the exact dimensions to cut the pipe are given. The allowances for the fittings have already been taken into account. Be sure the Tee fittings on the outside ends of the spokes are horizontal, as shown. Be sure the Elbow fittings on the outside of the top and bottom spokes are facing the same direction.

2. On your coil of copper tube, mark a line that divides the coil in half. Coils of copper tube usually have slightly damaged ends, or the ends are straight instead of curved. Avoid those ends but use as much of the coil as you can. You should be able to get seven semi-circular arcs. Mark those arcs in order from 1 to 7, largest to smallest, so you can assemble the spiral in the same order. Pull the coils of tube straight up until there is room enough to use your tubing cutter, and cut all the sections.

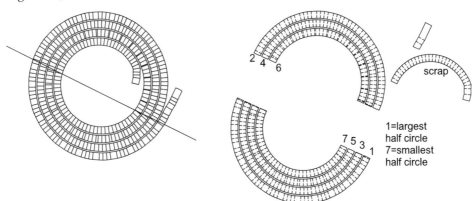

1=largest
half circle
7=smallest
half circle

3. Put the center pole in a vertical position. You can pound a piece of rebar in the ground and put the center pole over it, or put rebar or a dowel in a vise and put the center pole over it.

4. Starting at the bottom, assemble each of the seven half circles into the fittings, in order, from largest to smallest. The pieces of curved tube may seem to be slightly off size, but you can easily adjust the soft copper tube by hand to go into the fittings on the center pole.

Spiral using Straight Pipe and Elbows

about 6"W x 48"H

Materials List

• 1 pipe cut to **d42.5** for the center pole (see assembly notes before cutting)

• 22 pipes cut to **d6** for all pipes in the spiral

• 1 pipe for the bottom of the pole, cut to **d6**, or longer if you will be sinking it in the ground.

• 4 pipes cut to **d3**

• 26 90° Elbow fittings and 1 Tee fitting

Assembly Notes

1. Assemble five **d6** pipes with Elbows at each end as shown.

2. Assemble five "U" shapes from **d6** pipe as shown.

3. Assemble 2 "J" shapes from **d3** and **d6** pipe as shown.

4. On a flat table, assemble the five **d6** pipes with elbows to the "U" shapes in the main spiral, and the "J" shapes at either end. Use a square to check the angle shown and make sure it is 90°. Check the distance from one corner of a spiral to the same corner of the next spiral. The corner-to-corner distances should be the same from spiral to spiral, about 8½". Use pieces of lumber along the sides if necessary to keep the "U" shaped pieces upright while you work. Notice that the two "J" shapes are not angled like the spiral pipe assemblies. They will be horizontal when the project is standing vertically.

5. Check the actual dimension needed for the center pole. **d42.5** is given as a guideline, but your assembly may require a little more or less. Cut and assemble the center pole to the spiral, and the pipe at the bottom of the center pole, remembering to make it 12" to 18" long if it will be buried under ground.

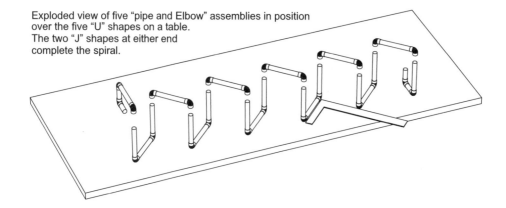

Exploded view of five "pipe and Elbow" assemblies in position over the five "U" shapes on a table.
The two "J" shapes at either end complete the spiral.

136

Spiral using Bends and Elbows

about 13"W x 78"H

Materials List

- 1 pipe cut to **d72** for the center pole (see assembly notes before cutting)
- 2 pipes cut to **d6.375**
- 1 pipe cut to **d6** or longer for the bottom of the center pole
- 10 pipes about 30" long with 90° bends in the middle
- 12 90° Elbow fittings and 1 Tee fitting

Assembly Notes

1. Bend 90° angles in the middle of 10 pipes about 30" long. Use a jig or framing square as shown below to mark the legs on 8 pipes at 12-5/8" (actual measurement). On the other two pipes, mark one leg at 12-5/8" and one leg at 6-5/16". Cut the pipes at your marks.

2. Lay the 8 large bent pipes on a table so they are all oriented like an "L", and assemble an Elbow fitting to only the top end of each "L". Assemble the fittings so they face the direction shown in the illustration below.

3. Assemble all the bent pipes with attached Elbows to each other on a table as shown in the previous project, except for this spiral each "L" connects directly to the next one, with no extra pipe in between. The distance between corner elbows on this spiral should be about 18".

4. Assemble the shorter "J" shaped bent pipes to either end, noticing that they are not angled like the spiral. They will be horizontal when the project is standing vertically. Then attach the **d6.375** pipes to the ends of the "J" pipes.

5. Check the actual dimension needed for the center pole. **d72** is given as a guideline but your assembly may require a longer or shorter pole. Assemble the center pole to the spiral, and add a pipe for the bottom of the center pole.

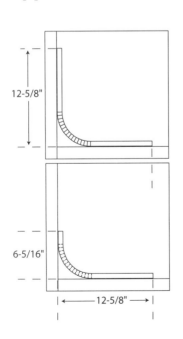

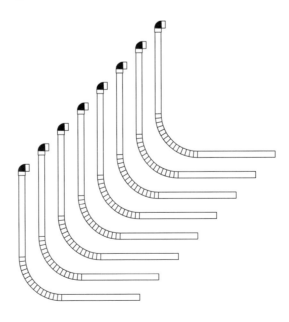

CHAPTER 14 *Other Garden Projects*

In This Chapter	Besides Trellises, copper pipe can be used to make many other useful structures for your garden. This chapter includes projects for row cover supports, cloches, plant stands, and plant supports.

Row Cover Supports and Cloches

Row cover supports and cloches are intended for supporting garden fabrics, sun shade fabrics, or plastic sheet. You can use them to protect plants or seed rows from early or late season cold, from sun, or from wind and rain.

To fasten the fabrics or plastic to the pipes, you can use a vinyl pipe called "funny pipe", sold in the irrigation or sprinkler supply area of the home centers, usually near the plumbing supply area. Cut a piece of this pipe about 4" long, slit it open along one side, and then use it as a flexible clamp over the fabric and pipe. It fits over ½ inch diameter copper pipe, not ¾ inch. A simpler method of securing the fabric is to use large "binder clips" available at any office supply store. The clips are steel and will rust, but they work well for the purpose.

Plant Supports

Plant supports are simple structures designed to hold up long stemmed plants. Without some sort of support, many tall flowering plants will simply fall over during high winds or stormy weather. An example would be gladiolus. If you don't support the fan of leaves, the plant will probably lean or fall over. Later, the plant sends up a long flower stalk which will also break or fall over if it is not supported.

For really tall plants, you can make up some simple pole supports (See page 65) and stand them up in each corner and/or around the edges of your main support. The bottom end of the poles should be pushed a few inches into the ground. To hold the poles upright, wrap electrical wire around the poles and the plant support where they meet. You don't have to use copper pipe for these verticals. You can accomplish the same goal with any handy "pole" such as bamboo or cedar stakes.

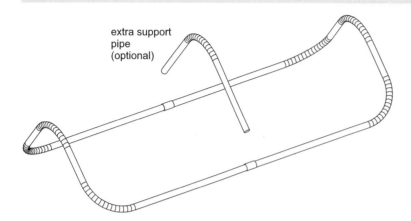

extra support
pipe
(optional)

Row Cover Support One by Bending

about 36"W x 8"H x 18"D

Materials List

- 1 10' pipe, 1 bent pipe (optional)

- 2 straight couplings or 2 Tee fittings

This is an easy compound bending project.

The entire procedure for this project is given in the Bending chapter, on page 48.

A variation that will provide an extra support pipe is to bend another pipe, cut it to size, and use Tee fittings to connect the two halves and the extra pipe.

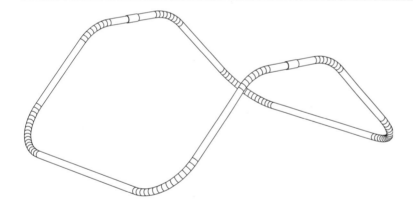

Row Cover Support Two by Bending

about 24"W x 10"H x 28"D

Materials List

- 1 10' pipe

- 2 straight couplings

Assembly Notes

1. Cut the 10' pipe in half. Mark 14" from each end of each pipe. Face one end of the pipe and put the start mark on your conduit bender directly over the 14" mark. Bend the pipe straight up in the air to 90°. Do the same at the other end of the pipe. Now you have a "U" shaped pipe.

2. Mark 2" from each end of the pipe. Stand facing one end of the pipe with your conduit bender. The first two bends you made should be lying flat on the floor. Put the start mark on the conduit bender directly over the 2" mark. Bend the end up to 45°. (Note **45°**, not 90°). Then bend the other end the same way.

3. Make the same bends on the other 5' pipe. Use straight couplings to connect the two halves.

Row Cover Support Hoops about 36"W x 12"H

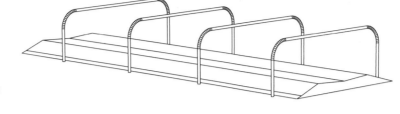

Materials List

- 1 10′ pipe for every two hoops

A very easy bending project.

Cut a 10′ pipe in half. Mark 9" in from each end of each pipe. Face the end of the pipe when bending, and make a 90° bend at each mark. This bending technique is completely described on page 45.

For this project, the way you arrive at the 9" measurement is as follows: you want the pipes to be 36" apart after bending. You add 6" to that length to get the distance between start marks, which is 42". You center the 42" between the ends of the 60" pipe that you start with, which leaves 9" at each end.

Support these hoops with rebar in the ground inside each leg.

Long Cloche Support

about 72"W x 16"H x 16"D

Materials List

- 3 pipes cut to **d72**
- 4 pipes cut to **d6**
- 4 pipes with 90° bends
- 6 Tee fittings

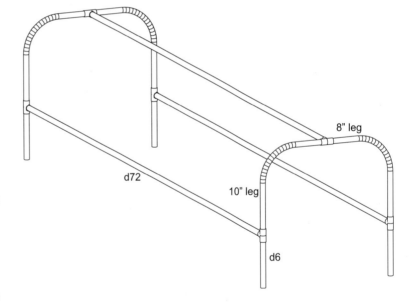

This project is easy to assemble. First make the two end pieces with Tee fittings facing outwards as shown, then assemble the long connecting bars between them.

You can make this project so it can be "knocked down" for storage. To do this, completely assemble the two end pieces and cut the connecting bars. To use the cloche, use hose clamps to secure the connecting bars to the end pieces as shown on page 34. Remove the hose clamps at the end of the season, and all the parts will store flat.

You can modify any dimension of this project to meet your needs. You can reduce the length by making the connecting bars shorter. The 90° bent pipes can have longer legs on one or both ends to make the support taller or wider. Or the bent pipes can have shorter legs to make the support shorter or narrower.

Walk-In Cloche Supports about 140"W x 79"H

This project makes a very large, light duty support for garden fabrics or plastic sheet so you can provide a little extra protection to larger plants or a whole garden early or late in the season. The structure is not strong enough to support a snow load, so don't try to keep it up all winter if your area gets snow.

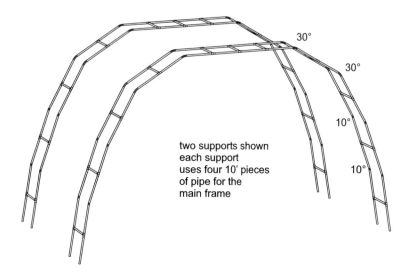

two supports shown
each support
uses four 10' pieces
of pipe for the
main frame

Materials List for each support

- 4 10' lengths of pipe
- 11 pipes cut to **d12**
- 22 Tee fittings

Assembly Notes

Mark each of the four 10' pipes at 24" intervals. Put 10° bends at the first two marks, and 30° bends at the second two marks.

Lay the bent pipes next to each other, and mark halfway between each bend. Cut the pipes at the marks, and reassemble them with the **d12** cross bars and Tee fittings. Join the two halves of the support at the top with a Tee fitting and a **d12** cross bar.

You can increase the strength and stability of this project by putting another Tee fitting in the top center cross bar and adding a center pole that goes to the ground, supported by rebar in the ground. You can also add Tee fittings and long connector bars to connect two or more cloche supports.

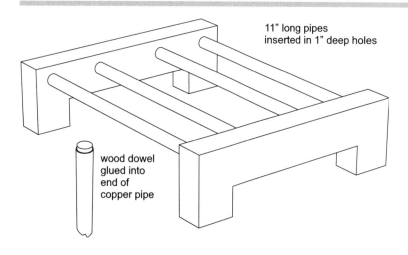

11" long pipes
inserted in 1" deep holes

wood dowel
glued into
end of
copper pipe

Plant Stand with Wood about 12"W x 3.5"H x 12"D

This project consists of four or more pipes supported by two end pieces made from treated wood or plastic lumber. You can make the pipes and the end pieces to whatever dimensions you need.

To fasten copper pipe to wood, you can glue wood dowels in the ends of the pipes with epoxy or exterior grade construction adhesive. Allow the glue to set. For ½ inch diameter pipe, drill 5/8" holes about 1" deep in the end pieces where you want the pipes to go. Screw through the end pieces into the wood dowels. You can counter bore the screw holes in the end pieces and fill the holes with plugs if you wish.

Three Level Plant Stand
about 24"W x 21"H x 18"D

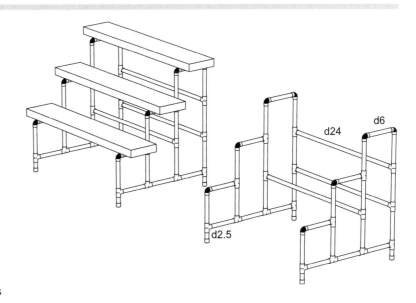

Materials List

- 3 pipes cut to **d24**
- 30 pipes cut to **d6**
- 4 pipes cut to **d2.5**
- 8 90° Elbow fittings
- 18 Tee fittings
- 4 end caps

If you make this project as shown, you can use treated 2x6, 1x6, or plastic lumber to make the shelves. The shelves are part of the structure of this project and should be screwed to the pipe frame from underneath with brass screws. Make the **d24** pipes to another size if you wish. Add another leg at the bottom center of each side to increase the strength.

Plant Shelves with Wood

about 51"H, length and depth variable

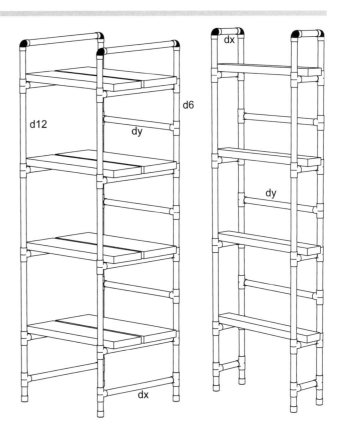

Materials List per stand

- 6 pipes cut to **d12**
- 20 pipes cut to **d6**
- 4 pipes cut to **d3**
- 12 pipes cut to **dx** (see below)
- 3 pipes cut to **dy** (see below)
- 4 90° Elbow fittings, 26 Tee fittings
- 4 end caps

The **dx** dimension is 1" more than the width you want your shelves to be, and the **dy** dimension is 2" less than the length of the shelves. Get your shelving material first, and cut **dx** and **dy** to match the shelves you want. The shelves should be fastened to the pipe frame with brass screws from underneath.

The narrow version shown would not be very stable by itself. It should be securely fastened to a wall or other support with copper straps around the back cross bars.

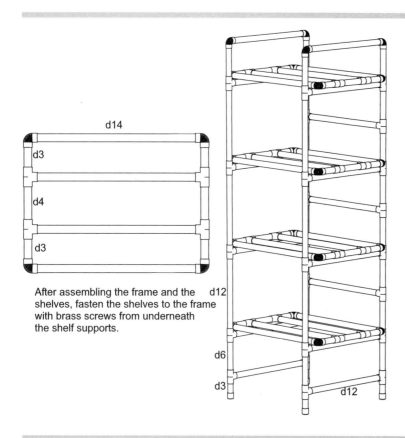

d14

d3

d4

d3

After assembling the frame and the
shelves, fasten the shelves to the frame
with brass screws from underneath
the shelf supports.

d12

d6

d3

d12

Plant Shelves with Pipe about 51"H x 14"W x 12"D

Materials List for the frame

- 21 pipes cut to **d12**
- 20 pipes cut to **d6**
- 4 pipes cut to **d3**
- 4 90° Elbow fittings
- 26 Tee fittings, 4 end caps

Materials list for each shelf

- 4 pipes cut to **d14**
- 2 pipes cut to **d4**
- 4 pipes cut to **d3**
- 4 90° Elbow fittings
- 4 Tee fittings

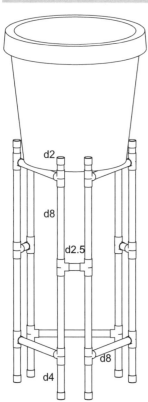

d2

d8

d2.5

d8

d4

Plant Stand about 12"W x 22"H x 12"D

Materials List

- 18 pipes cut to **d8**
- 6 pipes cut to **d4**
- 3 pipes cut to **d2.5**
- 6 pipes cut to **d2**

If you make this plant stand to the dimensions given above, it will support a pot with a bottom diameter of about 9 to 10 inches.

You can also add a table top as shown in the next project to support smaller pots.

If you want to support a larger pot, make the three large vertical rectangles but without the **d2.5** connecting pipes. Stand the verticals up and arrange them to a size that will hold your pot. Then determine the length needed for the connecting pipes, remembering that each end of the pipe needs to enter the Tee fitting by
3/8" (if using ½ inch diameter pipe).

Table Top Stand about 9"W x 26"H x 9"D without top

Materials List

- 2 pipes cut to **d13**
- 1 pipe cut to **d10.5**
- 6 pipes cut to **d8**
- 1 pipe cut to **d5.5**
- 3 pipes cut to **d5**
- 2 pipes cut to **d3**
- 6 pipes cut to **d2.5**

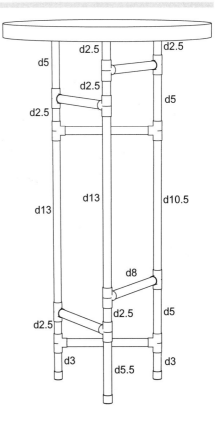

The top as shown is 16" diameter.

You can use exterior plywood for the top, and fasten it to the copper pipe by screwing into dowels in the pipe as shown on page 142. Then cover the top with mosaic tiles.

If you have or buy a top and don't want to screw through it, you can fasten 1/4" exterior plywood to the pipes, then screw through the plywood into your table top from beneath.

Plant Support Hoops

Plant support hoops can be used to support any type of tall plants, such as gladiolus, that may get knocked over during winds or storms.

You can make a "grid" from wire or string inside the hoops to keep the plants separated. In addition to supporting plants growing up through the center ring, you can support plants growing around the ring by tieing wire or string to the legs or hoops and then around the plants to be supported.

Give the support hoops themselves good support by putting a leg over a piece of rebar sunk in the ground.

These can be made any size you wish, to match the plants you need to support. The dimensions shown are just examples.

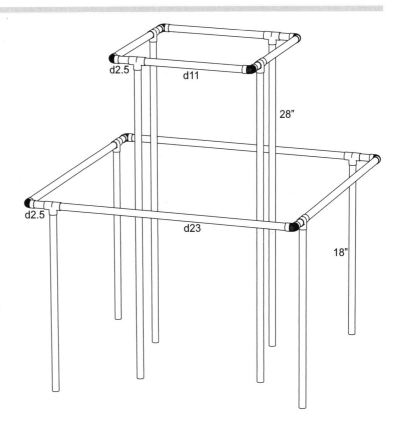

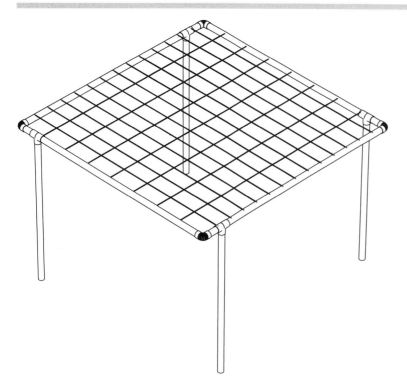

Plant Support Hoops with Mesh

The home centers sell many types of materials in their fencing or outdoor departments that can be used to make a grid within your plant support hoops.

They will usually have plastic coated wire fencing and plastic mesh fencing materials.

You can cut these materials to the size you need, and fasten them to the pipe hoops with plastic wire ties, found in the electrical department of the home centers.

If the mesh size is too small, you can use wire cutters to cut out some of the wires and make larger size openings.

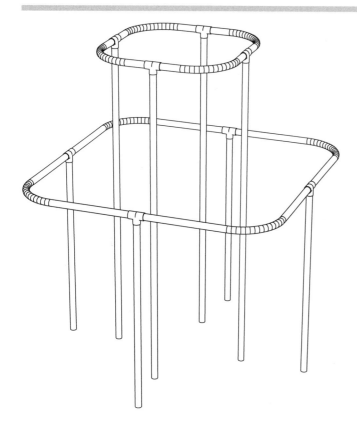

Plant Support Hoops by Bending

Another variation of the plant support hoops, this time made by bending pipe. The bent pipe eliminates a lot of fittings and joints.

Each support hoop consists of 4 pipes bent to 90°, assembled to each other with Tee fittings, and supported with legs in the same Tee fittings.

If you want supports that you can "knock down" for storage at the end of the season, don't solder the legs into the Tee fittings. Instead, secure them in place with hose clamps as shown on page 34.

CHAPTER 15

How to Support Copper Pipe Garden Ornaments

Once you have made a trellis, arbor, or other structure, you need to give it permanent support in your landscape. This chapter shows you how.

Providing Support for your Projects

All the copper pipe projects you build will need some sort of support when you install them in your garden.

First, the project needs to support its own weight and the weight of any plants growing on it. You do this by sizing the pipe in your projects to match the intended use of the project. Use ½ inch pipe for most trellises and small arbors that will support annual vines. Use ¾ inch pipe for large trellises or arbors that will hold heavy perennial vines such as wisteria, trumpet vines, and some types of roses and clematis.

Second, your copper pipe projects need to stay in a fixed position. They may need to stand upright in a pot, stand upright in the ground, or stay in position against a wall or a fence.

And last but not least, your copper pipe projects also need to resist the considerable force of the wind. This force can be very significant when a large leafy vine covers a trellis or arbor.

This chapter will show many ways you can support your copper pipe projects.

Supporting Pot Trellises or Growing Poles in Pots

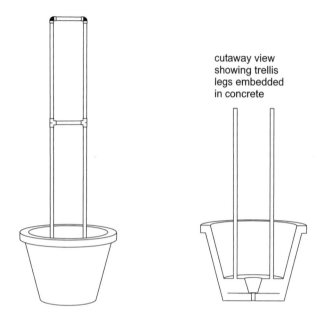

cutaway view showing trellis legs embedded in concrete

Many vines are quite happy growing in pots, and can easily climb a six foot tall pole or trellis fastened in the pot.

But if the pole or trellis is not firmly secured in the pot, it may fall over from its own weight and the additional weight of the plant. And if it is secured, a strong gust of wind may blow over both the trellis and the pot.

Here is a solution for both problems: use rocks, brick, or concrete to fasten the trellis in the pot. This also adds weight to the pot to prevent the pot from tipping over in the wind.

To use Brick, Rock, or Concrete Pieces:

1. Use a larger, wider pot or planter than you normally would. If you expect to grow a large perennial vine, consider using a concrete pot instead of a light plastic pot.
2. Solder angled "feet" at the bottom end of your pot trellis, as shown on page 66.
3. Stand the pot trellis so the legs are on the bottom of the pot.
4. Add heavy rock, brick, or broken concrete over the legs. Try to wedge both the legs and the uprights in an immovable position.
5. Add your potting soil and plant.

To use Poured Concrete:

Follow through step 3 above, then:

4. Secure the trellis in a vertical position. One handy way to do this is to set up a stepladder over the pot and trellis and tape the trellis to the stepladder.
5. Use a plastic funnel to plug the pot's drain hole. Tape it in place. The funnel will form a new drain hole through the concrete.
6. Mix and pour a 2" layer of concrete in the bottom of the pot, covering and embedding the trellis feet, and around the funnel, but not filling the funnel.
7. Wait 24 hours, then remove the funnel. Punch out any bit of concrete that may have seeped into the pot's drain hole.
8. Cover as much of the pot as you can in a large plastic trash bag and wait a week for the concrete to cure completely, then add your potting soil and plant.

Supporting Portable Trellises

You can make portable trellises that you can position next to plants that need support, whether the plant is in a pot on your deck or a plant in your garden. Maybe you want your peas to have a trellis early in the season, and some Morning Glories to have a trellis in a different part of the garden later in the season.

Here's how you can do it:

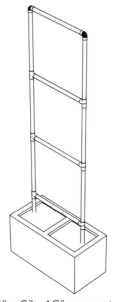

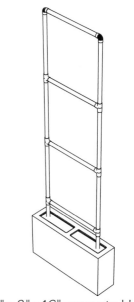

1. Obtain a 8"x8"x16" concrete block with holes from your home center.

2. Make or use a trellis that spans the distance between the holes.

3. Put the concrete block on a level surface. Add a ½ inch layer of damp sand to the holes, and tamp or pack the sand down firmly with a piece of 2x4 lumber or similar tool. The sand will seal the bottom of the concrete block temporarily so concrete does not leak out.

8" x 8" x 16" concrete block   *4" x 8" x 16" concrete block*

4. Secure the trellis in a vertical position.

5. Mix and pour concrete into the holes in the concrete block, surrounding the trellis legs and filling the concrete block to the brim.

6. Wait 24 hours before disturbing the block or the trellis. Then keep the concrete damp for a week so it can develop maximum strength. One way to do this is to put the concrete block in a plastic garbage bag.

You can use your portable trellis just by setting it on the ground near the plant you want to support. For even more support or resistance to wind gusts, you may wish to bury the block in the ground.

You can also use a 4"x8"x16" concrete block if you plan to bury the block in the ground. This is a good size for putting a "semi-permanent" trellis close against a fence or wall.

Tip	The concrete block can be painted with any exterior grade latex paint if you don't care for the gray concrete.

Supporting Free-Standing Structures with Rebar

A free-standing trellis is one that has no support from a fence, wall, or overhead beam.

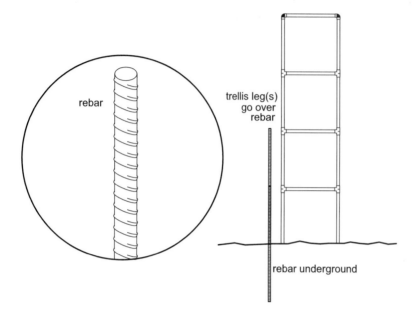

One way to support a free-standing trellis is to use lengths of rebar (concrete REinforcing BAR). One end of the rebar will be in the ground, the other end will be hidden inside the legs of your trellis. Home centers usually sell cut lengths of rebar in the same area as the sacks of concrete mix, or they may be able to cut longer lengths to the size you need. You can cut rebar with a hacksaw if you need to. A tubing cutter will not cut rebar.

This method is suitable for trellises up to about 4 feet tall.

1. Use ½ inch rebar for ½ inch pipe. ½ inch rebar fits inside ½ inch plumbing pipe nicely. Use straight lengths at least three feet long.

2. Use a sledgehammer to pound the rebar into the ground at least a foot deep, where one of the legs of your trellis will be. Make sure you pound it in as vertically as you can – a leaning rebar will result in a leaning trellis.

3. Put the open end of one leg of your trellis over the rebar and slide the trellis down to the ground. Mark the spot where the other leg touches the ground. This is where you will pound another piece of rebar.

4. Pound in the second piece of rebar, then slide your trellis over both pieces of rebar. There should be at least a foot of rebar in the ground, and a couple feet of rebar within the legs of your trellis.

Supporting Free-Standing Structures with Fence Posts

Another way to support a free-standing trellis is to use fence posts, also known as "T" posts because of their shape. This type of post is typically used to support a welded wire fence. (A "T" post is **not** the round, galvanized post used to support chain link fences.)

Fence posts are available in the fencing section of your home center. They are usually green in color, and after installation next to a trellis, don't really draw attention to themselves. You can also paint the fence post brown, to match aged copper, if you wish. Fence posts are usually available in 4 foot or 6 foot sizes. Use the largest one you can for maximum support.

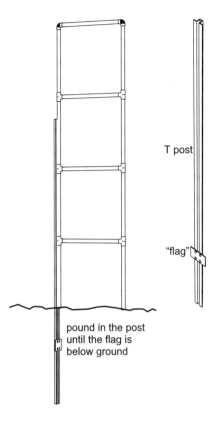

T post

"flag"

pound in the post
until the flag is
below ground

1. Decide where you want your trellis to be, and mark where one leg of the trellis will be.

2. Use a sledgehammer, and pound the post into the ground at the mark, so that the flat flag on the post is at least 6" underground. Keep the post vertical.

3. Position the trellis next to the post. If possible, position the trellis so a vertical pipe runs within the fence post channel. Mark the location of the other leg of the trellis.

4. Pound in a second post.

5. Put the trellis in position and use heavy copper wire to tie the trellis to the fence posts.

Supporting Trellises by Burying the Legs

Shorter trellises of about 3' above ground height can be supported by burying about 12" to 18" of the legs underground.

Remember that if you intend to support a trellis in this fashion that you need to add that much extra length to the legs. If the legs are too short, you can use a straight coupling to add another piece of pipe to each leg.

Don't try to pound a copper pipe or trellis into the ground. You will only dent or bend the pipe. Instead, dig a narrow hole for each leg, insert the trellis, and then backfill and tamp the dirt back into the hole.

If you have the right type of soil, you may be able to blast a hole with water pressure from your garden hose connected to a straight piece of pipe. You can get plumbing fittings at the home centers to connect a garden hose thread to a threaded fitting or a threaded pipe.

See page 152 for how to add extra underground support to prevent single-pole trellises from turning.

Using Trellises to Help Support Each Other

Almost any arrangement of two or more trellises fastened together will provide much better resistance to wind than one trellis by itself. You should still use rebar or fence posts to fasten one or more of the trellises to the ground.

Some advantages to this method are that you can make different arrangements of trellises from season to season or from year to year. Plus, if you want to store the trellises over winter instead of leaving them in your yard, they will stack flat.

The illustration gives some ideas for arranging trellises to support each other. Bind the trellises together by wrapping with heavy gauge copper wire or plastic coated electrical wire wherever the trellises meet.

Extra Underground Support

Some projects shown in this book, such as the spirals, have a single center pole. You can make the center pole long enough to go underground for support, but a single pole by itself won't be enough to prevent the spiral from turning or twisting above ground. By adding another leg to the support pole and burying it underground as shown in the illustration, you can provide better support and prevent the center pole from turning.

Supporting Trellises on a Deck

Tall trellises on or along a deck should have support at both the top and bottom. If you have no way to support a tall trellis at the top, such as an overhead beam or part of a pergola, you should either make a frame for the trellis as shown later in this chapter, or use a smaller portable trellis as shown earlier.

Fitting trellises to a deck requires that you think about how you are going to attach the trellis at the top and bottom, take accurate measurements, and then build custom trellises to fit the space. Once you have your trellises, here is one way to attach them along the edge of a deck, without drilling holes in your deck other than a few screw holes:

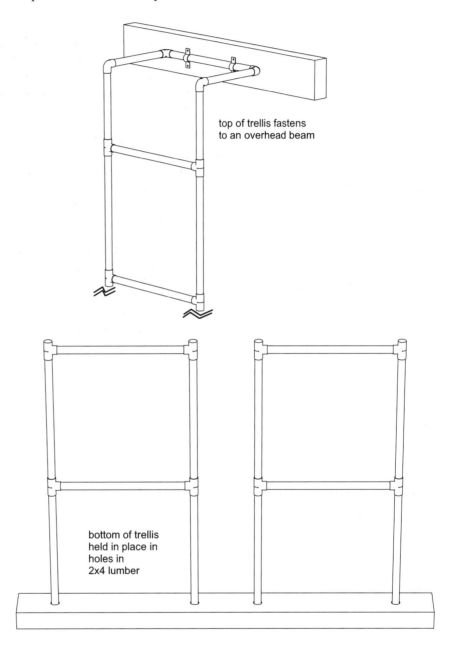

top of trellis fastens to an overhead beam

bottom of trellis held in place in holes in 2x4 lumber

1. At the bottom, the trellises should have straight pipe legs, with end caps. At the top, you may need to build in some horizontal legs in order to reach an overhead beam while still keeping the trellis vertical.

2. Obtain a piece of 2x4 pressure treated wood, or a piece of plastic lumber, whichever matches your deck.

3. Lay out the spacing of your trellis legs and the spacing between the trellises on the wood.

4. Drill ¾" holes (for ½" pipe) for the trellis legs through the wood, on your layout.

5. Fasten the wood piece on the edge of the deck or wherever you want the trellis.

6. Insert your trellis legs into the holes and stand the trellis up vertically.

7. Fasten the top of the trellis to the overhead beam with copper straps. Add horizontal extenders to the trellis as shown, if necessary. Use brass screws for corrosion resistance.

Supporting Trellises Against a Fence or Wall

Against a wall, use a trellis that is supported mostly by the ground. Kept it vertical by attaching the top of the trellis to the fence or wall. A trellis not resting on the ground, but supported entirely by fasteners going into a fence or wall, will be under tremendous strain if you try to grow large plants such as roses, pyracantha, wisteria, etc.

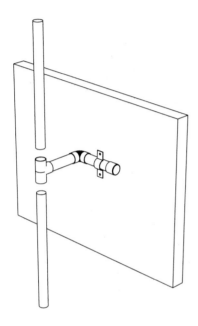

You can fasten a wall trellis to the ground with rebar in the same way as fastening a free-standing trellis to the ground, except you can use shorter lengths of rebar. Six inches in the ground and six inches within the trellis legs should be sufficient. See the information earlier in this chapter.

At the top of the trellis, you normally want some "stand off" distance from the wall, so that the trellis is not flat against the wall. When you make a trellis intended to go against a wall, you will need to plan ahead and add horizontal "legs" while building the trellis. Then you can fasten the legs to the fence or wall with copper pipe strap as shown in the illustration.

Another method that doesn't require you to build legs into your trellis is to fasten pressure treated wood or plastic lumber spacers to the wall. Then fasten the trellis to the spacers with copper pipe strap.

Use the strongest fasteners you can – good size brass screws for wooden fences or walls, or expansion fasteners with brass bolts for concrete or brick mortar joints.

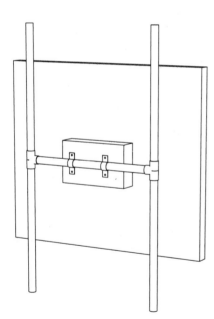

Maximum Support for Large Trellises or Windy Areas

If you plan on using large free-standing trellises or arbors, or if you live in a location that is exposed to high winds during thunderstorms or at other times, you should take special precautions when installing the structures.

First, use common sense. If summer storms normally blow in from the west, orient your trellis so the **narrow** edge faces west. If you get strong winds sometimes from the west and sometimes from the south, compromise and orient the trellis so the narrow edge faces southwest.

Then, provide strong support into the ground on each side of the trellis. Six foot long "T" type fence posts on each side of the trellis, as shown on page 151, can provide good support for trellises or arbors up to about eight feet tall. The fence posts will not be noticeable after the trellis fills in with greenery.

For the maximum support for a large trellis, you may want to consider making a frame from 4x4 and 2x4 lumber and embedding the posts of the frame permanently in the ground in concrete footings, as shown in the illustration.

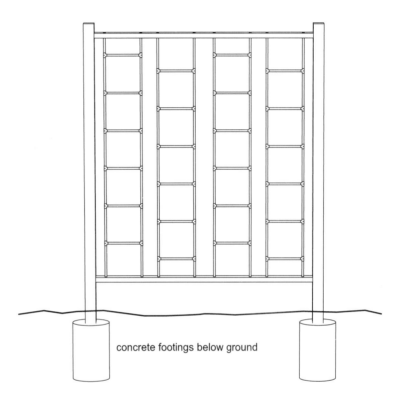

concrete footings below ground

CHAPTER 16 *Plants for Poles, Trellises, Obelisks, and Arbors*

In This Chapter

Now that you have a trellis or other structure that can support vining plants, here are some of the plants you might like to try.

Vining Plants

Any plant described as a "vine" or a "climber" will do well on a trellis or similar support. Here I will describe my experience with some of the more popular or useful vining plants. If you check your seed catalogs or local or mail order nurseries you will find many more.

Tip

Hummingbirds consider many types of vines to be among the most attractive nectar producing plants. If you have tried without success to attract hummingbirds with a feeder, try growing a few of the vines mentioned as being attractive to hummingbirds. You may find that you get constant visitors or even permanent summer guests.

In the following listing, an "annual" is usually bought as a small plant or grown from seed in the spring, flowers in the summer months, and dies by fall or winter. A "tropical" is a plant native to a much warmer part of the world than the US, but can be grown in most of the US during the summer months. It will probably die at the first frost. A "perennial" is usually bought as a small plant during spring or fall, will flower during the spring and summer months, and can survive from year to year. If you are interested in perennials, you should know your gardening "zone", which determines which plants can survive a typical winter in your area. Your local nurseries will also be able to tell you which plants will do well and survive in your area.

All the vining plants described here except ivy need "full sun". If you don't put them where they can get at least 6 hours of direct sun every day, they may not do well, or may not flower.

Almost all the vining plants described here do not need any help from you in order to climb a trellis. Most of them will naturally wrap their stems or leaf stalks around any suitable diameter support. Poles and trellises made from ½ inch copper pipe are ideal.

Cardinal Climber *(Ipomoea x multifida)*. Cardinal Climber is a fast growing annual vine. It has small, bright red, trumpet shaped flowers. The leaves are deeply notched. Even in a small pot, Cardinal Climber can grow 8 feet tall or more in a couple of months. You can also let it climb a smaller trellis and then cascade down when it gets to the top. The flowers are very attractive to hummingbirds. For this reason, consider starting some Cardinal Flower seed in trellis pots every month or so from early spring to mid summer. As the flowers come into bloom, you can move the pots to your deck or patio and enjoy both the flowers and the birds.

Cardinal Climber is typically available only by seed. Check the mail order seed sources (See page 169) if you can't find it locally. One odd thing is that books usually list Cardinal Climber and the related "Cypress Vine" *(Ipomoea quamoclit)* as two distinct plants, and photos of the two plants show them as having different leaf shapes. But seed companies sometimes refer to them as being the same, and their seed packs may even say something like "Cardinal Climber Cypress Vine".

Cardinal Climber flowers are similar to Morning Glories in that each individual flower blooms just once, for most of a day, and then fades out. The next morning, more flowers open and repeat the cycle.

Once you have some Cardinal Climber, it will produce hundreds of flowers, which in turn will produce hundreds of seed pods. Just save as many pods as you want, and you will never need to buy seed again. Start Cardinal Climber seed the same as for Morning Glory.

Chilean Glory Flower *(Eccremocarpus scaber)*. I'm cheating with this one, in that I haven't actually grown it yet. But it is related to Crossvine and Trumpet Vine, has flowers that are mentioned as being attractive to hummingbirds, and comes from a part of the world where hummingbirds spend the whole year. Sounds like a good one to try out!

Glory Flower is a vine, and is only available from seed as far as I know. Check with the mail order seed sources for a company that has it. Depending on your growing zone, Glory Flower may be hardy or you may need to start new plants each year.

Clematis *(Clematis species)*. There are dozens and dozens of different varieties of Clematis, too many to describe in much detail here. If you are interested in a perennial vining plant with loads of flowers, capable of climbing a small pole on your deck or covering a large arbor, then there is a Clematis for you. Check with local or mail order nurseries for descriptions of the different types. Some Clematis are attractive to hummingbirds, but this information is not usually given in catalogs. Your best bet to finding the ones that hummingbirds like may be to do an Internet newsgroup search on "hummingbirds and clematis" and see what experiences other people have had. The very popular "Jackmanii" Clematis is mentioned as being attractive to hummingbirds, but I have no first-hand experience with this particular one (yet).

Crossvine *(Bignonia capreolata)*. Crossvine is a large perennial vine related to Trumpet Vine, but is not nearly as vigorous or invasive. You can plant Crossvine in the ground near a large trellis or arbor, which it will cover in a year or two, and not worry about the plant invading other parts of your garden. Crossvine can be grown in a large pot with a large pot trellis, but it will do better in the ground.

Crossvine does not make a dense cover of leaves - it will allow light through a trellis or let you get a little bit of a view through a trellis. You can leave it like that, or grow another plant like a Clematis on the same trellis to fill in the spaces. Crossvine produces many orange-yellow-red streaked flowers during the summer and is attractive to hummingbirds. The plants will often produce "waves" of flowers, alternating with periods of rest.

In the fall after flowering is finished, Crossvine leaves turn a very attractive deep burgundy color.

Honeysuckle *(Lonicera species)*. Honeysuckles have a bad reputation because one type, Japanese Honeysuckle *(Lonicera japonica)*, is a serious invasive pest in many parts of the country. Once it gets a foothold in a hedge or along a fence from birds dropping the seeds, you will probably never get rid of it. Japanese honeysuckle is sold in nurseries, but avoid it. Use one of the following types instead.

Gold Flame Honeysuckle *(Lonicera x heckrottii)* is an attractive plant with reddish flower buds that open to reveal yellow flowers. With a pot trellis, Gold Flame makes a shrubby sort of vine and won't get too big. In the ground it will grow much bigger and can cover a large trellis.

Trumpet or Coral Honeysuckle *(Lonicera sempervirens)* is a good choice if you want to cover a very large structure. It will pretty much cover any size support you care to provide for it, and then some. A good choice for an arbor.

Some honeysuckle stems will naturally find their way around a support like a trellis, but many stems will grow away from the trellis and the plant can start to fall over or turn into a bush. Every week or so, you can tuck the longer shoots back into your trellis frame in order to keep the plant growing up and within your trellis.

Honeysuckles are perennials, and are very attractive to hummingbirds. They bloom from spring to frost, sometimes with a few "rest periods" in between blooming periods. Some honeysuckles have a very strong perfume (which is why people grow Japanese honeysuckle), and some don't. If the fragrance is important to you, ask your nurseryman or read the catalog descriptions to find out.

Ivy *(Hedera species)*. Many ivies such as the common English Ivy *(Hedera helix)* send out long stems with aerial rootlets. The rootlets turn into real roots if they come into contact with moist soil. The rootlets turn into "holdfasts" if they contact dry bark, wood, or brick. The holdfasts allow the ivy to climb walls or trees. You can certainly grow ivy in a pot trellis, or set up a trellis for ivy in the ground, but the holdfasts will not cling very well to copper pipe and you may need to help the plant climb by tying the stems to the trellis.

Unlike the other vines mentioned, ivy does well in shade or part shade. Ivy does not flower until it gets very tall. Ivy has nothing of interest to hummingbirds.

Mandevilla *(Mandevilla)*. Mandevilla is a showy tropical vine, with thick leathery leaves 4-6 inches long, and large pink flowers. Mandevilla is very adaptable - you can grow it in pots or in the ground, you can use a single pole trellis or a larger trellis. On a single pole, you can tie each stem to the pole as the stem gets long enough. After the stem is tied once, it will usually start to wrap itself around the pole from there on. The leaves and flowers will naturally arrange themselves around the pole without help from you.

Mandevilla is available at most local nurseries in the spring, in anything from small pots without many flowers (cheap), to large pots with a bamboo trellis and lots of flowers (expensive). To save money, buy a small, healthy looking plant early in the season and put it in your own trellis pot. With full sun and fertilizer, you will have the equivalent of the expensive plant within a month or so.

In pots, Mandevilla likes fast draining soil. Try using three parts regular potting soil and one part sand or perlite as your potting mix. Mandevilla also likes fertilizer. Without fertilizer the plant will simply stop blooming. With fertilizer you will have a constant flower show from spring to first frost. I use one-third strength of a liquid fertilizer such as a "Bloom Booster" every time I water, with good results. Rain in my area usually provides a dose of fresh water every couple of weeks or so and prevents any fertilizer build up.

Many books say that Mandevilla is attractive to hummingbirds. My backyard birds (ruby throats) will poke at the buds before they open, but after the flowers bloom the birds ignore them!

Moonflower *(Ipomoea alba)*. Moonflower is an annual vine closely related to Morning Glories. The main practical difference is that the large, creamy white flowers open late at night, not during the day. Sometimes the flowers can get "fooled" by cloudy days or cool weather, and you might catch one open during the day. But most of the time, you will need to stay up late to see the flowers blooming!

Moonflower is grown from seed using the same method as for Morning Glories. Moonflower is not attractive to hummingbirds.

Morning Glory *(Ipomoea purpurea)*. Morning Glories are very popular, fast growing annual vines. There are dozens of different types available as seeds. Morning Glory flowers open soon after daybreak, and fade out by early afternoon. Individual flowers only bloom once, but the plants produce hundreds of flowers in a single season. Most types of Morning Glory can easily climb a ten foot trellis in a month or so. On a smaller trellis, you can let the vines reach the top, fall back down, and start climbing up again. This can create a very bushy effect within a few months.

Starting the seeds for Morning Glory is somewhat tricky. Most seed packs will tell you to "nick" the seed or soak it overnight. I would ignore the advice about "nicking" - it is unnecessary, and more likely to damage the seed than do anything useful. Instead, just put the seed in a glass of water 24 hours before you intend to sow it. The seeds will swell up and break through the hard seed coat all on their own.

My experience with sowing most Morning Glory seeds is that about half of them will sprout, and about half of the ones that sprout will turn into a vigorous plant. So you may want to sow about four times as much seed as the number of plants you actually want, and weed out the weak ones. Once you have a vigorous plant, stand back! With full sun, warm temperatures, good soil, and water, a Morning Glory can climb a trellis taller than you in just a few weeks.

Morning Glories don't really have anything to offer hummingbirds. But sometimes birds that are unfamiliar with Morning Glories, especially red Morning Glories like "Crimson Rambler", will make many attempts to find nectar in the flowers. This can be an interesting way to tell if the birds you see in your yard are "regulars" or "visitors". The regulars will soon learn to ignore Morning Glories. Visitors may check out many flowers before they realize that they are wasting their time!

Rose (climbing type) *(Rosa species)*. A climbing rose is a very attractive and wonderful smelling plant. It can produce many hundreds of blooms from spring to frost.

However, a climbing rose is probably not the best choice for a trellis, or even the largest arbor. A vigorous climbing rose can produce dozens of very long thorny canes in its first season, and within a few years can overwhelm almost any structure. Many people think of putting a climbing rose on an arbor, but if you do you will have a constant chore of trimming back the thorny branches so that they don't catch on your clothes or skin.

In my opinion, a better use for a climbing rose is to cover a large brick wall or side of a house that you don't need to walk near. You might consider a simple trellis type structure attached to the wall or house, to provide something to tie the canes to.

Trumpet Vine (aka Trumpet Creeper) *(Campsis radicans)*. Trumpet Vine grows wild and is invasive in many parts of the South. During the summer months, you can see its deep green foliage and bright red, tubular flowers along almost any stretch of country fence, at the edge of woods, or climbing telephone poles.

In your garden, you may want to think twice before you put Trumpet Vine in the ground. It can send out very long roots and start plants far away from the mother plant. Once it gets established it can be very hard to get rid of - any bit of root can start a whole new plant.

That said, Trumpet Vine can be a very attractive plant in a large pot with a sturdy, securely fastened trellis. A large concrete pot with a one foot wide, 6 foot tall trellis or obelisk would be ideal. The vine can get much larger than that, but you can keep it trimmed within bounds. You can also try training Trumpet Vine into a "standard". See the listing for Wisteria for more information on standards.

Mail order nurseries now offer several varieties of Trumpet Vine that they claim produce more flowers and are less invasive than the wild type, so you may want to check those out.

Trumpet Vine is a perennial and is very attractive to hummingbirds.

Wisteria *(Wisteria species)*. Wisteria is a very large perennial vine that produces hanging blue or purple flowers in the spring or summer.

Like Trumpet Vine, Wisteria is an extremely vigorous grower and can be very invasive if you plant it in the ground. Many people with Wisteria in the ground wish they had never heard of this plant - it can send runners just under the soil surface 20 feet in all directions, and start new plants anywhere and everywhere in your yard.

But, it also makes an attractive choice for a large pot with a large trellis. Or you can put the large pot near a pergola and let the plant cover the pergola for summer shade. Wisteria can also be trained into a "standard" - only one main stem is allowed to grow, and the top of the plant (about six or eight feet tall) is trimmed once or twice a year to maintain the shape of a small tree. The main stem will develop into a small, self supporting "tree trunk" within a few years. A pot with a well supported single pole makes a good support for training a standard.

Wisteria is not attractive to hummingbirds.

How to use Trellises to Attract More Hummingbirds

The hummingbirds you see in your yard may be mature male or female, or immature birds. Females and immature birds will more or less coexist with each other. They may temporarily chase each other away from their favorite flowers or have short squabbles, but they will usually keep coming back.

Male birds can be very territorial, and may constantly try to prevent any other bird from using the flowers in their territory. They may spend the entire day just sitting at some favorite spot, keeping an eye on their territory, with only brief intervals of feeding. If a male bird has a good view of your whole back yard, it may keep every other hummingbird in the neighborhood from using any flowers, even though it doesn't use them himself!

You can keep a male bird from claiming everything as its territory by limiting its view - the bird won't attack what it can't see. One way to do this is put plants attractive to hummingbirds all around your house. Each side of your house then becomes a possible new territory, and there probably aren't that many male birds in your immediate area that can stake their claim.

Trellises and arbors provide another way you can make separate areas in your yard. If you set up several trellises or arbors along the length of your backyard for instance, each one becomes a barrier that prevents a single bird from claiming everything. Even if you have a powerful male bird that rules one area, other birds will be able to sneak in where the male can't see them.

If you get a particularly obnoxious male bird, try putting out a feeder for him where **you** want him to be. The bird will most likely show a lazy streak, and spend all his time hanging out near the never ending food source. The rest of your flowering plants will be fair game for other birds as long as you put the feeder for the male where he doesn't get a view of the rest of the yard.

I personally think it is much more interesting to watch hummingbirds visiting flowering plants rather than feeders. Plus, feeders seem to make the birds lazy or even "addicted", and feeders make you do a lot of work filling the feeders and keeping them clean. If you want birds to always visit a certain spot such as your deck or patio or outside a certain window, you can provide plants they like in trellis pots, as shown in this book. Because the plants are in pots, you can rotate fresh pots to those spots as new plants come into bloom.

Other Hummingbird Plants

The plants in this section are not vines, don't need a trellis, and actually have nothing to do with trellises or arbors. But, I have found that the best way to attract hummingbirds to my yard is to have a wide variety of plants that they like in constant bloom. The birds may come first for these plants and then start visiting your vines, or they may find the vines first and then get interested in everything else you offer. Your vines may take a "rest period" and stop blooming for awhile, but some of these plants may be in bloom during that time. Any way you look at it, if you enjoy hummingbirds, having lots of flowering plants that they like is the best way to keep them coming back.

This is by no means an extensive list. Many books, catalogs, and web sites can point you to dozens of additional plants, some of which may do better in your part of the country or with the conditions in your yard.

Canna *(Canna species)*. Canna is a very tropical looking plant, getting about five feet tall with very large leaves and bright colorful flowers held high above the greenery. Canna looks best and will attract hummingbirds best if used in a group, but a group of Canna can take up a lot of space. If you have a lot of empty, sunny space you want to fill in with an interesting plant, this could be a good one. If you don't have lots of space, other plants would be more suitable.

The plant designers are hard at work on Canna, coming out with all sorts of fancy leaf shapes and colors, and different colored flowers. The trouble is, the nectar that hummingbirds like seems to get bred out of the fancy plants. For hummingbirds, stick with the most common everyday old-fashioned Canna, with deep green leaves and bright orange flowers.

Canna is started from roots planted in the early spring. Canna roots are often available like spring bulbs at garden centers and nurseries. If Canna is not hardy in your area, you can dig up the roots every fall and store them in peat moss in a cool but not freezing place until the next spring.

Cardinal Flower *(Lobelia cardinalis)*. Cardinal Flower gets about two feet tall and develops long flower stalks with small bright red flowers. Each stalk will keep producing flowers for a month or so. Cardinal Flower is a little bit unusual in that it prefers and flowers well in a "part sun" or "part shade" location. It likes lots of moisture in the soil and is a good choice for growing in a damp spot.

Cardinal Flower is a perennial, and is usually bought as a small plant at a local or mail order nursery. You may need to do a little calling around to find a local nursery that has it. Cardinal Flower will slowly spread from new offsets at the base of the plant each year. It will also self sow and start entirely new plants if you let the seeds develop.

Gladiolus *(Gladiolus species)*. Gladiolus flowers, especially red ones, are attractive to hummingbirds. Gladiolus is grown from bulbs that you plant out in early spring. Your local nurseries and home centers will most likely have displays of many types of spring bulbs at planting time. Gladiolus bulbs will multiply and can be dug up and saved from year to year, so you may only need to buy bulbs once.

Gladiolus plants have long flower stalks that can reach a height of five or six feet. Plan on giving the plants some support early in the season, and again when the flower stalks start to grow, or they will almost certainly blow over on a windy day.

Like Canna, gladiolus now come in a wide range of fancy hybrids which may not have the nectar that hummingbirds are looking for. If you plant gladiolus specifically for hummingbirds, stick with the most basic "old fashioned" types and avoid the modern hybrids.

Ipomopsis (aka Prairie Cypress, Standing Cypress, Gilia) *(Ipomopsis species)*. Ipomopsis is a little known plant, but if you like hummingbirds you will like Ipomopsis. The whole plant is designed to attract hummingbirds for pollination. The leaves are very fine and small so that they don't get in the hummingbird's way. Ipomopsis sends up flower stalks about four feet tall, with tiny red tubular flowers all around each flower stalk. The flowers are so long and narrow that only a hummingbird can get to the nectar, so the birds don't get any competition from bees and butterflies. From watching hummingbirds in action, each flower must have lots of tasty nectar, because the birds just can't seem to get enough. Each individual flower only blooms for a day or so, but the whole flower stalk will stay in bloom for about a month.

I have never seen Ipomopsis in a nursery, so you will probably have to grow your own from seed. Most books list the plant as being a biennial or even a perennial, but my experience with one called "Skyrocket" is that it can be grown like an annual, which means it will flower from seed the first year and then die. Sow your first seeds indoors six weeks before last frost. Put outdoors after last frost. The young plants will grow very slowly until warm weather arrives, and then will put on a fast spurt of growth to about four feet tall, after which the flowers will start to open about early summer.

Ipomopsis does well in a big pot with very well draining soil, or in very loose sandy soil in the ground. See the information under Mandevilla, page 159, for a good potting soil mix. This is a native plant that can handle harsh conditions, so do not overwater or overfertilize. If you want plants in bloom all summer, start a new batch of seeds every couple of weeks from (about) February to May.

Ipomopsis stalks are narrow and delicate, and will fall over in a strong wind. Stake them with any type of small diameter bamboo or metal garden stakes as they grow. Individual copper pipe plant poles would be overkill for these plants, but you can put one plant pole in a large pot and then run wires or plant ties to each plant growing in the pot.

Ipomopsis seed is more expensive than more common flower seed. But after it flowers, it will set seed from each flower and you can save the seed for next year. I have not noticed any reduction in blooming time from letting the plants go to seed.

Monarda (aka Bee Balm) *(Monarda didyma)*. Most Monardas grown in garden soil in full sun will become the size of a small shrub, about 3 feet tall, in a few months time. The leaves are very fragrant and can be used to make teas. The flower heads are round, about 2" across, with many individual red flowers in each head.

Monarda is a member of the Mint family and can spread itself very vigorously by underground roots. You may want to grow it in a raised bed, large pot, or other "walled off" spot for this reason.

Nurseries have started offering pink Monardas and "petite" Monardas, but if your interest is in attracting hummingbirds, stick with the large red flowering types.

Monarda is perennial in most parts of the US.

Sages *(Salvia species)*. There are hundreds of types of sages. To make things simple, all you really need to know is that if a plant is called a sage or a salvia, and has red or purple flowers, then hummingbirds will like it. Common ones include "Lady in Red", Autumn Sage, Pineapple Sage, and Mexican Bush Sage.

Some sages or salvias are sold as "bedding plants" and don't get more than a foot or so tall. Hummingbirds usually prefer plants with flowers well off the ground, so you might have better luck with the short ones if you grow them in a hanging basket. Try putting short salvias in a basket or pot hanging from a trellis or arbor that hasn't filled in with a vining plant yet.

If you live in the eastern half of the US, try growing Autumn Sage, Pineapple Sage and Mexican Bush Sage. These plants flower very late in the season when ruby throat hummingbirds are migrating south, and the birds might just stop by your yard for a little snack.

Copper Pipe Details and Other Pipe Fittings

The information here is not necessary in order to build garden structures from copper pipe. But if you like to know all about the materials you work with, here is some detailed information.

Copper Pipe Properties

- Copper plumbing pipe that meets US ATSM standards is 99.9% pure copper.

- The copper most commonly used in plumbing pipe is deoxidized with phosphorus, and is technically referred to as type C12200 copper tube.

- This type of copper has a melting point of 1981° F.

Copper Pipe Types

The two types of copper plumbing pipe available at most home centers are referred to as "Type L" and "Type M". The following table shows the physical properties of each type.

	Nominal Size	Actual Inside Diameter	Actual Outside Diameter	Wall Thickness	Weight in pounds per linear foot
Type L	½	.545	.625	.040	.285
Type L	¾	.785	.875	.045	.455
Type M	½	.569	.625	.028	.204
Type M	¾	.811	.875	.032	.328

Note that the outside diameter of a ½ inch pipe is always .625", and the outside diameter of a ¾ inch pipe is always .875". This is so all ½ inch fittings fit any pipe called ½ inch, and all ¾ inch fittings fit any pipe called ¾ inch.

It is the inside diameter of the different types of pipe that is different. The different inside diameter results in a different wall thickness for each type of pipe. "Type L" pipe weighs more, and is more rigid and dent resistant than "Type M" pipe because it has thicker walls.

Other Fittings for Copper Pipe

REDUCER FITTINGS

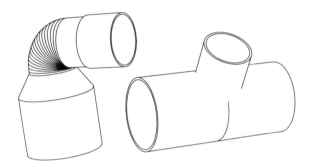

Reducer fittings allow you to assemble pipes of different diameters to each other. The most useful reducer fittings are shown in the illustration.

The ¾ x ½ 90° reducer Elbow on the left allows you to connect a ¾ inch diameter pipe to a ½ inch diameter pipe at right angles.

The ¾ x¾ x ½ reducer Tee on the right allows you to connect a ½ inch diameter pipe at right angles to two ¾ inch diameter pipes.

These fittings can help improve the looks of some larger projects. For instance, if you make a trellis entirely from ¾ inch diameter pipe, it can seem quite massive. If instead you make the main frame from ¾ inch pipe, but use reducer Tees to connect ½ inch diameter cross bars within the main frame, the trellis will have a more refined appearance.

UNUSUAL FITTINGS

The fittings shown for the projects in this book are those which are commonly available at most home centers and hardware stores. There are two other uncommon fittings which can come in handy with certain trellis designs you may wish to make. These uncommon fittings may only be available at a plumbing supply house, and you may need to special order even from them. The fittings are made from cast brass instead of wrought copper. You can solder them as you normally solder any other fitting, except that they will require more heating time with your torch. Be prepared to pay much more for these fittings than the common wrought copper fittings.

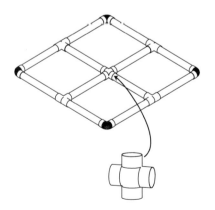

One such fitting is a "cross" or "sweat cross". It can connect 4 pieces of pipe at right angles to each other as shown in the illustration.

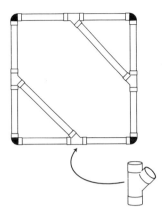

Another uncommon fitting is called a "45° Y". It can connect two pieces of pipe in line with each other, and a third pipe at 45° to the others, as shown.

NON-EXISTENT FITTINGS

If you build many copper pipe projects, you will many times wish that the fittings shown in the illustration were actually manufactured. Then you could build all types of corners, box shapes, and shelves without resorting to using Tee fittings and Elbows facing in different directions. But, plumbers do not need these fittings, so they are **not** made.

These "fittings" do NOT exist

Appendix B   *Sources*

In This Appendix   Check here to find sources for many of the tools, materials, supplies, or plants mentioned in this book.

Copper Pipe and Most Everything Else

Your Local Home Centers and/or Hardware Stores. The plumbing section of these stores will have copper pipe as well as all common fittings, tools and supplies for working with pipe, and pipe epoxy. Other sections of the stores will have conduit benders, electrical wire, construction adhesives, concrete mix, rebar, and cement blocks. For more specialized tools or fittings for pipe, check your local Yellow Pages under "Plumbing - Supplies" to find a plumbing materials distributor that caters to professional plumbers.

Seeds and Plants

This is a very short list of companies I have done business with several times. If you have Internet access, you can find many more seed companies and mail-order nurseries, as well as pictures and descriptions of most any plant. To find a source for any specific plant, try entering the plant name, either the common name or the scientific name, into an Internet search engine. Some of the results will be seed companies or nurseries offering the plant for sale.

If you search seed company web sites and you can't find a particular plant under its common name, try searching under the scientific name. Also, many sites will let you search for any part of a name or description, so you might try a search for "vine" if you want to see all the plants the site describes as vines.

169

Burpee Seed Co. The Burpee Catalog and web site offer many varieties of seeds that you can also find on in-store display racks, as well as others that are more unusual. Some seeds such as *Ipomopsis* are only available on the web site and are not shown in the catalog.

1-800-333-5808

http://www.burpee.com

Thompson & Morgan. The Thompson and Morgan catalog and web site offer seeds for many unusual plants not normally found on in-store seed racks. The web site offers many seeds not shown in the printed catalog, including *Eccremocarpus scaber*, Chilean Glory Flower.

1-800-274-7333

http://www.thompson-morgan.com

Wayside Gardens. A good source for perennial plants of all types, including vines such as Clematis, Crossvine, Trumpet Vine, Wisteria, and Honeysuckles if you cannot obtain them locally.

1-800-845-1124

http://www.waysidegardens.com

Your Local Garden Centers, Nurseries, and Home Centers. The best source to ask questions and find plants that will do well in your local area. The typical limitation is that they may only carry the most popular plants. If you want something a little out of the ordinary, you may need to grow from seed or buy from a mail-order nursery such as Wayside.

Internet Links

The Trellis Craft web site will be maintaining Internet links related to tools, supplies, and plants for trellises and trellis building. Visit:

http://www.trelliscraft.com

Trellis Craft Contact Information

I would be glad to hear from you – your questions, your comments about this book, photos of your projects, anything. If there is enough interest, I will start a picture gallery of projects on the Trellis Craft web site so you can share your projects and ideas.

Roger Beebe

Trellis Craft

PO Box 17000

Memphis TN 38187-1000

(901) 682-0961

roger@trelliscraft.com

INDEX

row cover supports 69, 139

S

saddle bends 107
safety 3
screws
    brass, reason for using 72
silicone 26
snake trellis 101
solder 14
soldering 17–21
    advantages of 10, 11
    complete technique 20
    de-soldering 21
    how to 17
    procedure 18
    safety 19
    solutions to problems 20
    supplies 13
    versus brazing 17
sources
    for materials 169
    for plants 169
    Internet sources 170
spiral trellises 135
square
    by measuring diagonals 30
start mark
    on a conduit bender 43
straight coupling 8
super glue 26
supplies 9–15
supporting projects 147–155
    against a fence or wall 154
    by burying the legs 151
    in a wood frame 155
    in windy areas 155
    on a deck 153
    overhead 153
    plant poles 148
    portable trellises 149
    pot trellises 148
    to prevent turning 152
    trellises to support each other 152
    with fence posts 151
    with rebar 150

T

T post 151
Tee fitting 7
    how pipes connect 37
teepee trellis 79
terms
    assembly terms 64

tools 9–15
    assembly 39
    reamer 13
    sand cloth 13
    wire brush 13
torch
    MAPP gas 11
    propane 11
    self-igniting 12
Trellis Craft
    address, phone number 170
    email address, web site 170
trellises 75–107
    fan trellises 103
    for pots 67, 68, 77
    for wood post 72
    how to support 147
    obelisks 125
    pillars 125
    portable 149
    snake trellis 101
    spiral trellises 135
    supporting against a fence or wall 154
    supporting in a wood frame 155
    supporting in windy areas 155
    supporting on a deck 153
    supporting overhead 153
    teepee trellis 79
    to attract more hummingbirds 161
    tuteur 134
    waterfall trellis 102
tubing cutter 9
    how to use 10
tuteur 134
type L copper pipe 5, 165
type M copper pipe 5, 165

V

vines 157
    attractive to hummingbirds 157

W

waterfall trellis 102
web site
    Trellis Craft 170
welding 17
wire brush cleaning tools 13
wood
    fastening to copper pipe 142, 145
wood frame
    for supporting trellises 155

Other Items of Interest

By the author of Trellis Craft:

THE CASTCRAFT MOLDMAKING AND CASTING GUIDES

by Roger Beebe. 236 pages, 8½ x 11. $39 including standard shipping.

Learn how to make molds and how to make 3-dimensional products by using molds. With a mold and the right casting material you can make products such as plaster decorations, ornamental concrete stepping stones, figurines, birdbaths, and fountains, resin cast figurines from "cultured marble", "bonded bronze", and "pecan shell resin", rubber pads, bumpers, and rollers, masks, ceramics, tin soldiers, chess pieces, candles, doll parts, puppets, fishing lures, and much more.

Includes up-to-date sources for all the materials covered in the Guides, plus sources for ready-made molds and other products and supplies related to moldmaking and casting. Includes 290 Sources for 216 materials! Plus — access to the Castcraft web site customer area with Internet links to over 210 sources.

THE CASTCRAFT MOLDMAKING TECHNIQUES VIDEO SET

by Roger Beebe. Set of two VHS tapes. Total running time 3½ hours. $39.95 including standard shipping.

This two-tape video set features demonstrations of making 8 different types of latex rubber molds (and their backup molds) from start to finish. Demonstrates a mold for a plaque, 3 ways of making glove molds for figurines, a larger figurine mold with a seam, a mold for a model with holes or "windows" through it, a mold for a model with extending arms, and a mold of a wicker basket.

Shows how to make backup molds from plaster, urethane plastic, and fiberglass. How to keep flat sections of molds from rippling. How to reinforce rubber molds. How to use filler to build up a mold faster. How to keep parts of the mold from shifting during use. How to turn plaster into a clay that doesn't set for hours, then sets hard. How to provide air vents. How to fill large and small undercuts. How to make legs to support the mold.

THE CEMENT BIRDHOUSE PROJECT GUIDE

by Roger Beebe. 18 pages, 8½ x 11. $12 including shipping.

This project is a printed manual that shows you how to make molds for cement birdhouses. The birdhouses feature a unique natural bark look, and a removable top for easy cleaning.

The project is intended for those who wish to make molds for birdhouses and sell quantities of birdhouses for profit. Making the molds will take several hours of your time, and approximately $120 worth of materials.

The guide is very detailed, with illustrations of every step of the moldmaking process. In addition, there are several full-size templates included so you can make parts easily.

Other items of interest

By others:

MOLDLESS CONCRETE POTTERY FORMING VIDEO

by Vida Cairns. VHS video. Running time 55 minutes. $43.95 including standard shipping.

This video was produced by Vida Cairns, who recently retired from running a cactus and bonsai nursery in Washington State. She shows you step-by-step how to make pots and planters like those illustrated. Her method uses no molds — just simple forms you probably have around the house, a spoon, and an inexpensive lazy-susan type turntable! No expensive equipment is needed.

You can make pottery in any color, any shape, and any design. Any size from Bonsai dishes up to Patio planters. Any texture, from smooth "ceramic" to rough "volcanic". The pots are durable and weatherproof for use indoors or out.

(Author's note: I made a pot from these techniques after I first saw the video over 10 years ago. The pot has been in use every year since and is still going strong.)

If your hobby is gardening, now you have a way to make your own unique pottery. Or include a handmade pot with plants you give to friends and family.

If you want to make planters for sale, it's possible to get a 20x return on your cost of materials! You can turn $10 worth of sand and cement into $200 worth of pots and planters — even more if you grow some plants to sell with the pots!

HOW TO BUILD A PIPE BENDING MACHINE

by Vincent R. Gingery. 48 pages, 5½ x 8½. $10.95 including standard shipping.

This book shows you how to build a hand operated, table top bending machine capable of making tight bends in copper pipe, conduit, and thick walled rigid conduit, plus flat or square steel stock.

The bending machine you can build from this book is similar in design to machines that cost hundreds of dollars to buy new.

Building this bending machine requires a well-equipped shop. You will be cutting, drilling, and welding steel. Making the forming dies requires either a wood lathe or a drill press.

All orders to:

Trellis Craft

PO Box 17000

Memphis TN 38187-1000

(901) 682-0961

or www. trelliscraft.com

checks, money orders, Visa, and Mastercard accepted